BONSAI FOR ALL

The Complete Beginner's Guide
to Keeping Your Trees Alive

D1519142

RJJ Publishing

This book is dedicated to our little acorns.

Max, Hayley and Pippa

TABLE OF CONTENTS

INTRODUCTION

ALL JOURNEYS BEGIN WITH A SINGLE STEP

T he mere idea of starting out in bonsai can be very overwhelming. You may be worried about how much time, money, and effort goes into creating such a beautiful piece of living art.

The truth is that success in bonsai is attainable to anyone who is willing to learn, regardless of skill level or finances. This book is designed to take anybody from any background on the journey to learning how to acquire and maintain their first bonsai tree.

No matter where you are in the world, *Bonsai for All* will be your helpful companion and guide, teaching you everything you need to know to get you started on your blossoming bonsai journey. If you take your time and follow the blueprint we have provided throughout this book, you too, will have the knowledge required to successfully acquire, care for, and maintain your trees for many years to come.

The Evolution of Bonsai

Although the word *bonsai* is Japanese, the art of growing miniature trees in pots originated in China as far back as 1,000 A.D.
The Chinese have always loved nature and gardening due to the
rich biodiversity in their country.

Japan began adopting Chinese cultural hallmarks, and the art of
bonsai became established.

The Japanese introduced Zen Buddhist principles in bonsai, and
the art was especially popular in Buddhist temples. As bonsai increased in popularity, anyone, from members of the ruling elite
to impoverished laborers, began practicing bonsai as a way to
practice their spiritual beliefs.

At the dawn of the 19th century, the term *bonsai* was officially
coined, and the religious aspect of the practice began falling away
to the crafting and design of the miniature trees. As the century
progressed, numerous books and catalogs were published detail-
ing the methodology behind the art. As the hobby grew, the first
bonsai shows were held where people could admire the tiny
works of art.

After the Pacific War, bonsai blossomed into a fundamentally
Japanese native art. Apprenticeship programs were common-
place, along with a great number of shows, publications, and
classes.

Despite its long history, bonsai can still be considered relatively
new in Western culture, with the first mention of bonsai trees in

China appearing in 1637. Japanese miniature trees made appearances at a number of fairs and conventions in the late 19th and early 20th centuries in the United States, as well as Western Europe.

As travel increased between the West and Japan, bonsai began to take root across the world. The art form continues to grow as enthusiasts learn more about bonsai, and the rise in interest has led to the creation of websites, discussion forums, and online clubs.

Bonsai is referenced in popular media, from movies and television to social media and literature. At this time, the number of bonsai enthusiasts is approximately 10 million people worldwide. That number is continuing to grow, and you are now about to join this global community of green-fingered enthusiasts!

What Will This Book Cover?

You will start by learning about the anatomy of a tree, as well as its growth cycles and natural habitats. You'll also gain a much better understanding of what makes a tree truly healthy.

You'll learn what makes a tree a bonsai, and you'll be introduced to the Japanese terms for the different sizes of trees. Don't worry! We'll use the Japanese names sparingly, and we've provided you with a handy glossary at the end of this book that you can always refer back to.

When you're comfortable with the basics, we'll show you how to choose your first tree. You'll see the different types of trees commonly used for bonsai as well as the different styles of trees that are available. If you're a beginner, you'll learn about the trees that are best suited to your skills, and we'll guide you on how to choose a reputable bonsai nursery.

You'll learn all about where to place your bonsai tree when you bring it home for the first time and how to look after it properly while it acclimatizes.

You'll need some tools to get started with bonsai, and we'll take you through it all. We'll give you options in different price ranges so that you can get what you need without breaking the bank! You may discover you already have tools laying around that are suitable for bonsai work.

We've dedicated a whole chapter to repotting because as your tree grows and develops, it'll need a bigger container. As with any tree, there are some precautions you'll need to take when repotting your bonsai. We've got you covered!

You know that watering your plants is essential and the same is true for your bonsai tree. We'll teach you how to listen to your tree so that you're able to water it effectively. We'll also talk about the dangers of over and under-watering, as well as the importance of good drainage.

Choosing the right soil for a bonsai tree gives even the experts some level of anxiety, but we'll take you through all the do's and don'ts! You'll learn about the different types of soil that are most suited to bonsai, as well as where to get it.

Your bonsai will need fertilizer, and we'll take you through the different types of fertilizers and the pros and cons of each. You'll learn about organic and synthetic fertilizers, when to introduce them to your tree, and we'll even discuss some of the latest developments in bonsai fertilizer.

Styling and shaping your bonsai tree is your goal as a bonsai enthusiast. You'll discover the different types of techniques and styles, as well as the best way to go about it. Pruning is another essential element of bonsai, and we'll take you through the best time to prune your tree to keep unwanted growth in check. You'll also learn how to go about pruning the different parts of your tree, from roots to new shoots and thick branches.

Wiring your bonsai tree is a quick and easy way to help it grow into your desired shape, but it tends to make people nervous. We'll go through the pros and cons of both aluminum and copper wire, and we'll take you through the step-by-step process of wiring your tree.

A nice thick trunk may be one of your bonsai goals, so we'll discuss how planting your tree in a bigger pot, or even in the ground, can help you to achieve that goal.

All gardeners will know that pests are a certainty, whether you have plants in the ground, pots, or in raised beds. Pests can cause huge amounts of damage to your bonsai tree, so we've got a whole chapter discussing pest control.

Protecting your tree from the elements, especially as the seasons change, will ensure it lives a long and healthy life. We'll show you how to protect your tree from wind, sun, and other seasonal elements.

You may be wondering if you should get a young tree, a more mature tree, or if you should grow your tree from seed. We'll discuss the pros and cons of each with you so that you can make an informed decision based on your budget, your skill level, and the time you have available.

We also have two great chapters on how to acquire trees for absolutely free.

Regardless of your skill level, joining a bonsai club is a great way to meet up with other bonsai enthusiasts, whether it's in person or online. Not only will a bonsai club give you a chance to interact socially, but you'll be able to share ideas and experiences with fellow club members, giving you the opportunity to hone your skills. We will discuss the benefits of this near the end of the book.

No matter which way you look at it, bonsai is both art and science. It's about growing and nurturing a living thing and appreciating the beauty that it offers.

Begin your journey into the world of bonsai, learn from the experts, and watch your tree thrive!

Are you ready to take your first step?

"Tall oaks from little acorns grow" –David Everett

CHAPTER 1

TREES 101

As you begin your bonsai journey, you need to start at the very beginning by taking the first foundational step and learning about bonsai trees, their anatomy, and their health. This will help you to gain a greater understanding of what will follow in the book and will set you up for success.

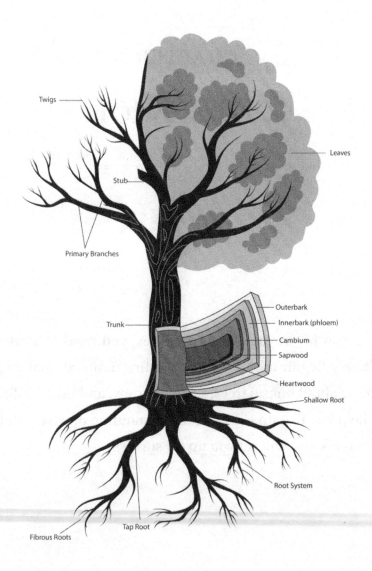

Basic Anatomy of a Tree

Roots

The root system of a tree helps it to absorb nutrients and water from the ground. They also help anchor the tree to the ground and store nutrients for the winter months when resources are scarce.

The root system is made up of large perennial roots which last year-round and smaller feeder roots that have a much shorter lifespan. The roots are most abundant in the top three feet of soil, and they extend outwards at least as far as the circumference of the leaf growth above. This helps the roots to absorb the water that drips down from the leaves when it rains.

Trunk

A tree trunk's primary function is to transport the water and nutrients absorbed by the root system to the branches and leaves and is made up of five layers.

1. **Outer Bark**

   The outer bark protects the tree from the outside world. It protects the tree from absorbing excess humidity and also helps it from losing moisture when the air is dry. It also provides insulation from both heat and cold and offers protection against pests.

2. Inner Bark

Also known as the phloem, the inner bark is the main transport channel for nutrients. It is constantly being renewed, and the layers of inner bark that have died move on to become part of the outer bark.

3. Cambium Cell Layer

This is the growing part of the tree trunk. It grows new bark and wood as it receives hormones known as auxins. Auxins are created by the tree's leaf buds in the spring.

4. Sapwood

Sapwood's main function is to transport water throughout the tree. As more sapwood is produced, the older inner cells lose their function and become heartwood.

5. Heartwood

Heartwood is the innermost supporting structure of the tree. It's made up of dead sapwood cells but won't deteriorate and lose its strength if the outer layers of bark remain intact.

Branches and Twigs

Branches and twigs grow from the trunk and serve as support for leaves, flowers, and fruit. They also transport nutrients between the trunk and the leaves.

Leaves

Leaves make food for the tree by photosynthesis and release oxygen into the atmosphere. Leaf shapes, with their ridges, lobes, and jagged edges, help to evaporate water during photosynthesis, minimize wind resistance, and help to shed rain that could cause leaves to decay if left standing.

What Makes a Tree Healthy?

A basic assessment of a tree's health is quick and easy to do just by looking at it. You can check the health of the tree by looking at the following:

Leaves

The leaves should be the right color for the season. It's important to remember that some trees have naturally occurring yellow or red leaves! The leaves shouldn't be oddly shaped or stunted in their growth, as this could be a sign of poor health. Wilting is another side-effect of stress on the tree.

Trunk

The trunk should be solid and hard, with no cracks or holes. The bark on the trunk shouldn't be loose or peeling. There are a few species of maple and birches that have this as a characteristic, but they are the exception to the rule.

Branches

Living branches are strong yet supple. Unhealthy or dead branches will break off easily and be unable to provide the support needed by the tree.

Observing these combined characteristics will give you a good indication that the tree you are looking at is full of life and in good health.

Coniferous vs. Deciduous Trees

The terms *coniferous* and *deciduous* are used to classify trees based on the shape of their leaves and how they produce seeds.

Coniferous Trees

Coniferous trees can be considered evergreen, as they have leaves all year. They do lose leaves, but these are quickly replaced, regardless of the season.

Coniferous trees can be identified as follows:

- **Leaves**

  Coniferous leaves are compact and pointed, resembling needles or scales. They're coated with a waxy layer and a cuticle, which helps them to retain water. The leaves are tough and hardy and not generally attractive to pests due to their taste. They can photosynthesize year-round, making them more resilient in extremely hot or extremely cold environments.

- **Reproduction**

  Coniferous trees are gymnosperms, meaning that they don't produce flowers but rather cones that house their seeds. As the cone matures and opens, the seeds are released.

- **Shape**

  Coniferous trees tend to grow very tall and straight, with their branches creating a triangular shape.

Deciduous Trees

Deciduous trees tend to have large, broad leaves which fall off the tree once a year, usually in the autumn and winter. The leaves then regrow in the spring.

Deciduous trees can be identified as follows:

- **Leaves**

  Because deciduous trees only have their leaves for a limited period, they need to maximize the surface area used for photosynthesis. This results in most deciduous trees having broad leaves. During the autumn and winter, the leaves turn yellow, orange, red, and brown before falling off the branches.

- **Reproduction**

  Most deciduous trees will flower annually and produce fruit containing their seeds. Flowering usually takes place as new leaves are growing, enabling pollinators such as bees and butterflies easy access to the flowers. The seeds are protected by a hard shell, such as the acorn, or by soft, fleshy fruit, like the peach. Seeds are usually spread by animals who feed on the fruit and dispose of the seeds.

- **Shape**

  Deciduous trees tend to grow outwards, optimizing their surface area to allow for photosynthesis.

The Exceptions to the Rules

As with anything in biology, there are a few exceptions to the rules, where trees can be both coniferous and deciduous.

The larch tree (*Larix laricina*) is probably the best-known deciduous conifer, naturally occurring in the colder regions of the northern hemisphere, such as Russia and Canada. The larch's needles turn yellow in the autumn before dropping off the tree.

Key Takeaways

- Trees consist of roots, the trunk, branches and twigs, and leaves.

- There are five layers in the tree trunk.

- The health of a tree can be seen in its leaves, trunks, and branches, and overall appearance.

- Although there are coniferous and deciduous trees, there are some exceptions to the rule.

Now that you've gone through some tree basics, let's focus our attention on the characteristics that define a bonsai tree.

CHAPTER 2

WHAT MAKES A TREE A BONSAI?

In this chapter, we will define the main characteristics of a bonsai tree. This will help you to see that creating a bonsai tree is easier than it looks. If you think of bonsai as an art form, you can compare it to painting. Many of the most revered painters learned the rules and then broke them while creating their masterpieces. In the same way, there is no right or wrong way to style a bonsai tree. You can use your creative streak to create something truly unique!

Throughout this book, we'll occasionally be using Japanese terminology. But have no fear! We'll keep it light, and we've included a handy glossary at the back of the book.

Defining Bonsai

As you already know, bonsai is a Japanese word, roughly translated it means "planted in a container." The first part, *bon* refers to a dish or thin bowl, while the second part *sai* means planted. The ultimate goal is to create a miniature but realistic version of a tree that is naturally occurring.

Bonsai trees are not genetically modified to be small, meaning that just about any tree can become a bonsai tree. This is done by pruning, wiring branches, and carefully controlling the amount of fertilizer the tree receives. As long as the tree species has a trunk, grows true branches, and can be grown in a container, it can become a bonsai tree.

Bonsai Sizes

Most bonsai trees are usually between two and three feet in height, with the largest at approximately four feet. Bonsai trees are classified according to their sizes.

- **Keishi bonsai:** thumb-sized, growing only about 1 inch tall. These extreme miniatures are extremely rare and difficult to maintain in the long term.

- **Shito bonsai:** known as fingertip bonsai, growing to a maximum of about 3 inches. Once again, they're difficult to maintain in the long term. They're usually grown for exhibitions before being replanted, allowing them to grow further.

- **Mame bonsai:** larger, but can still be described as miniature bonsai. They're known as single-handed bonsai trees because they can easily be moved with just one hand. They usually grow up to 6 inches.

- **Shohin bonsai:** the most popular size for many enthusiasts. Growing to approximately 8 inches in height, they make up about 80% of all bonsai grown.

- **Kifu Sho bonsai:** slightly larger, growing to 16 inches. Their larger size makes for a greater "wow" factor!

- **Chu bonsai:** commonly referred to as 2-handed bonsai trees, meaning that you will need 2 hands to move them. They grow to a height of about 24 inches.

- **Dai bonsai:** the biggest and are 4-handed, meaning that it would take 4 hands, or 2 people, to move them around. Their maximum height is roughly 40 inches.

Height classifications in bonsai are as much of an art form as the trees themselves. The classifications we discussed above aren't necessarily set in stone, and there are many enthusiasts who pay them no mind. The most important aspect of bonsai is the shape and style of your tree. Size is usually only a factor for someone who is buying an already established bonsai tree to look after or is looking to enter their own tree in an exhibition.

Characteristics of a Bonsai Tree

Bonsai can be best explained as a miniature replica of naturally occurring trees without obvious human intervention. There are a few characteristics that a bonsai tree needs to meet to be considered a true bonsai.

Firstly, the tree needs to look natural, although it doesn't have to be an exact replica of its full-sized counterpart.

A bonsai tree needs to be relatively small. This means that it should be easily transported from one location to another. It also needs to convey a sense of nature. The human touch shouldn't be obvious. In this way, the tree is able to represent something bigger than itself. Anyone viewing the tree should be able to connect with it on some level.

The ancient Chinese and Japanese held bonsai trees in high regard, and it was considered a great honor to view and care for a bonsai tree. We believe that the same respect should be given to the trees today.

Lastly, the bonsai tree should be seen as a miniature, portable slice of nature for all to enjoy. As it grows, the tree can mark the passing of the seasons and imitate a landscape favored by the artist.

CHAPTER 3

YOUR FIRST BONSAI TREE

Unless you have been given a bonsai tree as a gift, choosing your first bonsai tree can feel like quite a daunting task. To make it a little easier on yourself, you should ask yourself two simple questions.

Firstly, what type of trees do you like? Of course, all trees are amazing and beautiful, but try to be a little more specific when you're thinking about this. Do you like coniferous trees, or do you prefer deciduous ones? Do you like trees that flower? Perhaps you like trees with striking foliage or bark. The more specific you are, the more you can narrow down your choices.

You can always go online and start looking at images of bonsai trees. Create a collection of the types of trees that you find the most attractive. This will be the starting point for your bonsai journey.

Secondly, what size of bonsai tree would you prefer? We discussed the sizes of bonsai trees in the previous chapter. You need to take into account the space that you have available for your bonsai tree, whether it's indoors or outdoors. You will also need to think about your ability to move your tree around.

The Most Popular Beginner Bonsai Trees

When you're getting started, you may want to try your hand at one of the types of trees listed below. They're relatively easy to train, making them firm favorites among beginners.

Chinese Elm

The Chinese elm is one of the most, if not the most, popular beginner bonsai trees. Millions are sold every year due to their hardiness and tiny leaves. They are a great tree to style and are very forgiving, so a beginner can work on them with confidence.

The Chinese elm can be kept outside year-round in temperate regions, but care must be given, and protection from frost and extreme temperatures should be provided.

Juniper

The Juniper species has over 50 evergreen coniferous trees and shrubs that are ideal for bonsai. Its popularity among bonsai enthusiasts is due to the small leaves of the entire species. The small leaves work well with the miniature aspect of bonsai. The juniper is also a hardy tree that can handle extensive pruning.

Junipers grow best outdoors in bright, sunny light and need dry soil to thrive.

Pine

Pine trees are popular bonsai trees because they're tough and easily trained, working well with every bonsai style. The pine tree's most noticeable characteristics are its leaves, or needles, which grow in bunches, as well as its bark, which begins to flake as the tree gets older.

The most popular pine species are the Japanese black pine, Scots pine, and White pine.

Pine trees thrive in bright sun, and the soil needs to be completely dry before watering.

Japanese Maple

The Japanese maple is popular for its bright burgundy red leaves and its bark that becomes gray as it ages.

Japanese maples need plenty of water, especially during their growing season, requiring watering at least once a day or even several times per day in hotter climates.

Ginseng Ficus

The ginseng Ficus is a tropical tree that is great for bonsai begin-ners. The tree is characterized by its dark green, oval leaves, and striking aerial roots. It doesn't require as much light as other trees, so it does really well as an indoor plant. Just remember that, as a tropical tree, it needs a warm environment and moist soil.

Azalea

Azaleas are flowering shrubs, not trees, but some smaller varieties are more suited to be houseplants, growing to about 3 feet tall. Azaleas enjoy full to partial sun and dappled shade and need frequent watering. With the right care, you will be rewarded with its eye-catching white, pink, red, or orange flowers.

Dwarf Jade

The dwarf jade tree is an excellent tree for the bonsai beginner. It's a semi-evergreen softwood shrub that grows well indoors as well as outdoors in warmer climates. It's very similar to the common jade tree, but because it's a dwarf variety, its leaves are smaller, making it easier to prune.

The dwarf jade needs plenty of direct light and minimal watering to thrive.

Japanese Cherry Tree

In Japan, the cherry tree signifies friendship, and the different varieties of the tree make for exquisite bonsai. They're gorgeous, especially in the spring, and they're easy to train, making them popular among bonsai beginners.

They can spend the colder months indoors, but they need plenty of sunshine in the summer months, so it's best to move them outside. As the cherry tree blooms in the spring, you'll be dazzled by its pink or white blossoms.

Bonsai Styles and Shapes

After you've decided on a tree to begin your bonsai journey, you will have to start thinking about the style and shape in which you'll grow your tree.

As the art form developed, many different styles have been documented, with a great preference to have bonsai trees resemble their full-grown counterparts as much as possible. Although it's not necessary to stick to a particular style, it's always great to know how they've been classified. The different styles are best suited to different types of trees, which can guide you as you begin shaping your bonsai.

Let's look at some of the styles and shapes that you might consider as a beginner. We'll go more in-depth into styles and shapes in Chapter 9.

Formal Upright Bonsai Style

 The *Chokkan*, or formal upright style, is quite common, and it resembles naturally occurring trees that get plenty of light and don't have to compete with other trees for space. The trunk starts out thicker at the bottom and thins as it grows up. Branches should start growing at about the one-quarter mark of the trunk's height.

Informal Upright Bonsai Style

The *Moyogi*, or informal upright style, can be observed in nature and in bonsai. The tree trunk grows in an S-shape, with branches at each curve. Just like the formal upright style, the trunk is thicker at the bottom, tapering as it rises.

Slanting Bonsai Style

The *Shakan*, or slanting style, emulates a tree that has grown in the wind blowing mostly from one direction. In bonsai, the trunk should lean between 60 and 80 degrees from the ground, and the first branch should grow in the opposite direction of the slant, creating some visual balance. The root system becomes very well developed to support the slant of the tree. Despite the slant, the trunk must still be thicker at the bottom, tapering as it rises. This is desirable throughout all styles, and it's best to avoid inverse taper whenever possible. Inverse taper is where the trunk is thinner at the bottom but then becomes thicker toward the canopy.

Cascading Bonsai Style

The *Kengai*, or cascading style, will resemble a tree that grows on a cliff and bends downwards, usually as a result of falling rocks or snow. The cascading style is not easy to achieve in bonsai, as it goes against the tree's natural desire to grow upright. To achieve this style, trees are usually planted in taller pots, and the trunk is allowed to grow upwards for a while before being bent. The crown of the tree usually grows where the trunk was bent, and then alternating branches on the downward portion of the trunk create balance. Strong bends are created by using wire and we will teach you how to do this.

Buying Your First Bonsai Tree

Most nurseries or garden centers can have a selection of bonsai trees for sale at very reasonable prices, but they might not be of the best quality. Niche online bonsai stores or specialist bonsai nurseries will be priced higher, but the quality of the trees will be much better.

What to Look for When Buying a Bonsai Tree

When searching for your perfect bonsai tree, there are a few things that you will need to consider:

- Buy a tree that's best suited for where you want to place it. Tropical trees do very well indoors where it's warm, but they need plenty of light.

- With pruning and wiring, you'll be able to change the shape of your tree, but the trunk and root system are usually fixed. Be sure to choose a tree with a trunk that appeals to you.

- Keep your expertise level in mind when buying a tree. Buying a tree that's difficult to care for and having it die on you will leave you disheartened and financially out of pocket.

- Do your research before buying a tree to make sure that you have all the information you need. If you have been given a bonsai tree as a gift, take some time to learn about the species and its specific requirements.

- Look for signs of good health when buying your tree. It's much more challenging to bring a tree back to health, and failing to do so might crush your blossoming interest in bonsai.

Buying a Pre-Bonsai Tree

If you're feeling a little more adventurous, you may want to buy a tree that isn't a bonsai just yet. This means that you will have to train it to become a bonsai yourself. While this might pose a greater challenge, you will feel a huge sense of accomplishment!

A pre-bonsai tree is generally more cost-effective than an already-established bonsai tree. This is because the work still needs to go into it to create a gorgeous piece of art.

Developing vs. Refining Your Bonsai Tree

If you choose to purchase a pre-bonsai tree, when you get it home, you'll be tempted to put it in its pot immediately. This can be a mistake as it can cause your tree to grow up to 10 times slower than expected. Understanding the difference between developing and refining your bonsai tree will help you to make the right decisions about your tree at the right time.

Developing Your Bonsai Tree

When developing your bonsai tree, you'll be looking after it and developing its trunk and roots. You will need to make sure that these basics are strong and healthy before moving it into a bonsai pot.

When developing your tree's roots, you will automatically help the trunk develop. You can develop your tree's roots by leaving it in the container you bought it in until it becomes too big for the pot. Once this occurs, you can replant it into a bigger container. You can do this several times until you see that the roots are strong and healthy. A reliable indicator of strong roots is a trunk that thickens over time.

The next step in developing your tree's trunk is to work on its taper. This means that the bottom of the trunk needs to be thicker than the top. Once the bottom of the trunk is the thickness that you want, you'll start pruning branches toward the top of the trunk. You can leave the lower branches to grow, and each year, the bottom of the trunk will grow thicker and thicker.

Refining Your Bonsai Tree

You can start refining your bonsai tree once the trunk is thick enough and you've tapered it effectively. The trunk may be considered complete and will start showing other signs of maturity, such as cracked bark.

At first, you'll spend time working on the branches. You can remove any branches that you don't need, based on the style of tree that you want to achieve. You can also start pruning the remaining branches to the length you want. You may need some branches to be thicker, so you will follow the same technique as you did with the trunk. You can let the branch grow for a while and then cut back what you no longer need. The best time to do this is just before spring, depending on the species of tree.

As you see new branch growth coming through, you'll be able to start pruning and wiring your tree to shape the branches into your desired shape. We have chapters on both pruning and wiring coming up, so we'll discuss these techniques in further detail there.

Bringing Your First Bonsai Tree Home

Finally, you've made your decision, and you've purchased your first bonsai tree and have now brought it home!

Congratulations!

The Seven Fastest Ways to Kill Your New Tree

1. Not researching your tree's specific needs.

2. Placing your tree in the wrong location.

3. Under-watering.

4. Over-watering.

5. Repotting at the wrong time.

6. Styling and pruning at the wrong time.

7. Failing to protect your tree from pests and disease.

These are the most common mistakes we see beginners making time and time again. The aim of *Bonsai for All* is to help you avoid these common pitfalls and guide you along your path to bonsai success. So, please don't fear! By the time you have completed this book, you'll be equipped with all the tools you need to navigate through the hazards and care for your tree with confidence.

We will now start by looking at the various tools you will need to become familiar with to give your trees and yourself the best start along this exciting journey.

CHAPTER 4

TOOLS

As the art of bonsai grew and developed, tools were designed, created, and used specifically for bonsai. These tools help bonsai enthusiasts to make accurate cuts, leaving clean edges.

At first, you'll only need a few tools, but as you progress on your journey, you'll want to expand your collection to suit the needs of your tree. You don't have to buy top-of-the-line tools. There are a variety of tools available to suit every pocket!

Please don't be put off by the amount of equipment listed in the coming chapter. As a beginner, you won't need to purchase all the tools we talk about in order to get started. Each tool listed has a specific role to play, and it is useful to understand more about them.

Types of Tools

When you start researching the types of tools you may need for working on your bonsai tree, you will come across a huge variety. We've broken the tools down into three categories, namely cutting, maintenance, and repotting tools, and highlighted the ones that you'll need as a beginner.

Cutting Tools

- **Bonsai Scissors**

  Bonsai scissors are used for cutting and trimming finer twigs and branches. For more delicate cuts, you can invest in a pair of pruning scissors. A cheaper alternative when just starting out would be a pair of sturdy gardening shears.

- **Root Scissors**

  Root scissors are sturdier than the scissors used for cutting branches. A good pair of root scissors will help you to cut thicker, soil-covered roots while repotting your bonsai tree.

- **Leaf Pruners**

  Leaf pruners are used for buds and leaves. The sharp blades and pointed edges will result in clean cuts. They can also be used for fine twigs, branches, and roots.

- **Pruning Shears**

  Also, hand pruners, pruning shears can be used to trim back thicker branches that have plenty of twigs and leaves. The best shears have small jaws and neat cutters. These are a relatively cheap and versatile option for the bonsai beginner. We know of many successful bonsai enthusiasts who started out with nothing more than a handy pair of pruning shears. They also tend to be spring-loaded, so they are a great option for anyone who struggles with grip strength.

- **Wire Cutters**

  You'll be using either copper or aluminum wires to train your tree, so you'll need a pair of wire cutters. You'll have to choose a wire cutter based on the thickness of the wire you'll be using, and you can find these at your local hardware store.

- **Branch Cutters**

  There are three different types of branch cutters, namely concave, flat, and hybrid. Concave cutters have a curved edge, and they're designed to trim branch stubs on the tree trunk. Flat branch cutters serve the same purpose as pruning shears and can cut branches closer to the tree trunk. Hybrid branch cutters are a combination of concave and flat cutters. Hybrid cutters are generally a preferred option for many due to their versatility. All three are available in various sizes depending on your tree's dimensions.

- **Bonsai Saw**

As your bonsai tree matures and its branches become thicker, you won't be able to trim them with shears or scissors. You'll need to invest in a bonsai saw. The saw has a thin blade and sharp, fine teeth.

- **Pliers**

You'll use pliers for bending and tying wires as you train your tree. You can also use them for stripping the bark off the tree to create special bonsai effects such as Shari or a Jin.

Maintenance Tools

- **Soft- and Wire-Bristle Brushes**

A soft-bristle brush is used to remove any dirt from the surface soil. A wire-bristle brush, one with softer brass bristles, is used for cleaning the bark and branches of the tree and removing any algae growth from the pot while repotting. For a beginner on a budget, a soft-bristle tooth-brush will suffice.

- **Wound Sealant**

Wound sealant is vital for the health of your tree and is used on freshly cut areas and helps to prevent infection and repel pests.

- **Wires**

To train your tree, you'll use either copper or aluminum wire in varying thicknesses.

- **Watering Can**

The ideal watering can has a long nozzle that will allow you to reach into every corner of your pot.

- **Spray Bottle**

A simple spray bottle will allow you to mist your bonsai tree, and it can also be used to clean dirt off your pot.

- **Rust Eraser**

A rust eraser will help keep your tools in great condition.

- **Tool Sharpener**

A sharpener will help keep your scissors and shears sharp, allowing you to make more precise cuts with minimal stress to your tree. An ideal time to sharpen your tools is during the winter months. This can be done using a whetstone or a diamond sharpener. If these are not available, it is possible to sharpen your tools using sandpaper.

Repotting Tools

- **Chopsticks**

  You can use either bamboo or metal chopsticks to comb your tree's roots when repotting. You can also buy and use a root hook for this. Chopsticks can also be used to repack the soil once you have completed re-potting your tree.

- **Root Pruning Scissors**

  Root pruning scissors have much bigger blades than pruning shears. They're used for trimming and reducing roots when repotting.

- **Needle-Nosed Tweezers**

  These are specialized gardening tweezers with thin tips that will help you perform precision tasks such as handling delicate new growth, cleaning up after repotting, and picking out any bugs, weeds, or leaves.

- **Root Saw**

  A root saw looks very similar to a knife and is used to detangle and separate the roots of a root-bound tree while repotting.

- **Mesh**

  Mesh is important and is used to cover the drainage holes at the bottom of your pot. This will prevent insects from getting in and will stop soil from escaping when you water your tree.

Starter Tools

As mentioned earlier, it's not necessary to go out and purchase everything all at once. Remember that when you start out with bonsai, whether you get an already-established bonsai or a sapling, it will need plenty of time to rest and acclimatize, so the first thing you'll really need is a watering can.

As you start repotting and pruning, you'll need pruning shears or scissors, wire cutters, and a chopstick. As your tree grows and develops thicker branches, you can expand your collection of tools to include a concave branch cutter, a root cutter, and wound sealant before expanding to the full repertoire of tools listed in this chapter. However, your personal bonsai journey will dictate which tools you buy and when you choose to buy them. We believe everyone should enjoy caring for their bonsai trees without it costing the earth.

It's important to choose tools that you feel comfortable with. And remember, as you start out, some tools can be multipurpose!

Carbon vs. Stainless Steel Tools

As you begin shopping around for your set of bonsai tools, you'll realize that they're made of carbon steel or stainless steel. So, which is the best type for your needs? Here are a few things to think about.

Carbon steel tends to be a more affordable option than stainless steel. Carbon steel tools are also easier to sharpen, which is a great advantage if you're pruning and trimming your tree often. Although carbon steel tools are easier to sharpen, stainless steel tools are more durable and require less maintenance.

Stainless steel is also more resistant to rust, making it a firm favorite among bonsai enthusiasts.

To summarize, carbon steel tools are less expensive, and they're tough and durable if looked after correctly. Stainless steel tools are pricier, but they don't need as much maintenance.

Looking After Your Bonsai Tools

To ensure that your bonsai tools last long and work properly, you'll need to take some time to make sure that they're properly maintained. Here are a few things to consider:

- Clean your tools after every use. Don't allow dirt and debris to build up on your tools, as this will cause blades to stick and become blunt.

- If you have more than one bonsai tree, make sure to clean your tools after working on one tree and before moving on to the next. Should one tree be infected with pests or disease, you could easily make your entire bonsai collection sick. Some tree species are also toxic to others, so you could inadvertently kill a tree by not cleaning your tools properly.

- Always ensure that the edges are sharp. Pruning your tree with blunt shears will cause stress to your tree, slow down recovery time, and leave a nasty scar.

- Regularly oil your tools to help keep them rust-free. This is especially important in humid or coastal areas.

- Make sure your tools are completely dry before storing them. This will also help to keep your tools rust-free.

By looking after your tools properly, they will last longer, and your trees will also benefit!

Key Takeaways

- A variety of tools are used in the art of bonsai, but you can start off with just a few basic items.

- To get started easily, choose a few tools that can serve multiple uses. Shears are a cheap and multifunctional investment when starting out on your journey.

- Carbon steel tools are affordable but require more maintenance to keep them in top condition.

- Stainless steel tools are pricier but require less maintenance and last longer.

- It's important to keep your tools in great condition to ensure that they're able to serve you for a long time, as well as to ensure that they don't damage your tree when you're working with them.

Repotting your bonsai tree is an essential part of the process and one that can intimidate beginners. In the next chapter, we'll be going through the repotting steps, why it's done, and how to choose a new pot for your tree.

CHAPTER 5

REPOTTING

Repotting your bonsai tree is an important part of the process, and it can either help or harm your tree. It doesn't have to be a scary process, though! Repotting your tree at the right time with the right tools will result in a successful and healthy tree!

Reasons for Repotting

As you know, your bonsai tree grows in a very limited space, unlike its full-grown counterparts in nature. Within a few years, your tree will become root-bound, meaning that the roots will take up all the available space in the pot and become tangled. This results in a weak, unhealthy tree because the roots aren't able to absorb the nutrients and water that the tree needs.

In fact, in some species of trees, the roots will start pushing the tree out of the pot in an attempt to create more space!

Another reason to repot your bonsai is to make sure that the spread of fine roots at the soil line mirrors the spread of branches above. You want to encourage the finer feeder roots to grow to achieve this effect, and repotting will allow you to trim the thicker roots, encouraging the finer roots to grow. This will help you to create a strong *Nebari* (visible root flare seen at the surface).

When we refer to repotting in bonsai, we don't always mean placing it in a new pot. More often than not, repotting involves taking your tree out of its pot, pruning the roots, and then returning it to the same pot.

When to Repot Your Bonsai

Deciding on the best time to repot your bonsai tree can be tricky; there are no set dates on a calendar. Some highly experienced bonsai growers might advise you of certain seasons, but it's important to keep in mind that they're probably in a different part of the world with a different climate. The rule of thumb is to see what is happening with your tree before deciding to repot it.

You'll want to repot your tree as it comes out of its winter dormancy, and it starts showing signs of life again. In deciduous trees, this is usually when you can see the swelling of new buds on the branches. The best time to repot is when the buds are fully swollen, and the new leaves are just about to open up. This is the ideal time because the roots will have sent as many nutrients as possible to the new buds, so trimming the roots won't affect the health of the tree. If you repot too early, the buds won't be able to get the nutrients they need to produce more leaves. If you repot too late, the roots won't be able to absorb enough water to maintain the new leaves.

In coniferous, evergreen trees, it's a little different because the leaves are there year-round. You'll start seeing activity in coniferous trees a little later than in deciduous trees in the form of new leaves or needles. New root growth will also indicate that it is emerging from its dormancy, so you can lift the entire tree out of its pot to check the roots. Be mindful that some trees are wired into their pots. New roots will have white tips, so if you see that, you'll know your tree is ready for repotting.

There are other factors you can take into account when deciding to repot your tree. For example, when you're watering your tree, is the water immediately absorbed into the soil? If water isn't being absorbed, it may mean that the tree is root-bound, and you may have to remove the top layer of soil and some fine roots. If water is absorbed more easily after this step, you might be able to avoid repotting your tree. But if you see that the soil is compacted, then repotting will be your best solution.

Emergency Repotting

Sometimes accidents can happen. The elements can catch you by surprise; a strong gust of wind or a prolonged period of freezing temperatures can result in a cracked or smashed pot.

Don't panic, we've all been there, and there is a simple solution known as slip potting. This is when a tree is moved from one pot to another with minimal disturbance to the root system.

Prepare the new pot as quickly as you can and transfer the tree into it without cutting or damaging the roots. If you handle your tree with care and follow the repotting advice below, you will give your tree the greatest chance of surviving its ordeal.

How Often Should You Repot?

Younger trees will need to be repotted more regularly than older trees because they're in the stage of rapid growth. To create a bonsai from a sapling, you'll need to control the way the roots grow and how fast they grow, so regularly repotting it will help. Generally, younger trees can be repotted every two to three years, but repotting more regularly can help speed up the growth of the finer feeder roots as the thicker storage roots are trimmed back.

As opposed to younger trees, mature trees will need repotting far less frequently.

It's important to remember not to repot and style your tree at the same time. Each activity will cause your tree to use a lot of energy to recover, so by doing both at the same time or within a short time of each other, your tree will suffer. With some species, it's recommended to repot one year and style the next.

All About Pots

Choosing a new pot for your bonsai tree can be very exciting! Many bonsai enthusiasts go with their intuition when it comes to choosing a new pot, but there are a few guidelines that you should consider.

Masculine or Feminine Pots

It's believed that the pot complements the masculine or feminine features of your tree, so you need to decide if your tree is masculine or feminine. A masculine tree will typically have old bark, deadwood, a thick trunk, and dense branches. On the other hand, feminine trees tend to look more graceful with smooth bark and sparse branches. Once you've decided, you can choose a pot that complements those features.

- **Masculine Pots**

  Masculine pots are angular in shape, so you can choose a square, rectangular, or hexagonal shape. They're also very minimalistic, meaning that they're not painted and stick to a simple glaze in earthy tones. Finally, masculine pots give off a sense of severity, or heaviness, through their straight lines, angles, and the material from which they're made.

- **Feminine Pots**

  Feminine pots are more ornamental, so they will typically have more round edges and can be circular or oval. Feminine pots will have more colorful, decorative glazes and convey a sense of softness through their cheerful tones.

Remember, bonsai is an art form, and as such, your choice of pot and style will reflect your own individual tastes. These are more traditional guidelines, and you shouldn't be afraid to experiment. This is *your* bonsai journey, after all!

Size and Style

When choosing a new pot, you should keep two questions in mind. Firstly, will the new pot be big enough to accommodate the tree and its root structure? And secondly, how will it look with the style of your tree?

The size of your pot will be determined by your future plans for your tree. Do you want it to get bigger, or would you like it to stay the same size? If you'd like your tree to continue growing, then a larger pot will be the way to go, but if you want to keep it the same size as it is, you can stick to the same size pot. We will discuss this together in more detail in a future chapter.

Ideally, the length of the pot should be no more than two-thirds the height of your tree, and the width of the pot should be smaller than the widest spread of your tree's branches. Remember, you don't have to place your tree in the center of the pot. By placing your tree to one side, you'll have the space to add additional features to your bonsai to help it resemble its full-grown counterpart in nature, such as rocks.

How to Repot Your Bonsai Tree

To successfully repot your bonsai tree, you should follow a few simple steps to ensure that your tree recovers successfully.

Step 1: Removing the Tree From Its Pot

The first step is to remove your tree from its old pot. To remove it effectively, you'll need to separate the content from the sides of the pot. You need to ensure that you keep the pot steady while doing this so that you don't cause any unnecessary damage to your tree's roots.

As you lift the tree out, remember to loosen the roots from the bottom of the pot as well. If the tree is wired into the pot, be sure to cut the wires first before attempting to remove the tree.

Step 2: Preparing the Pot

It's important to replant your bonsai into a clean pot, so make sure to remove any dirt from the pot with a brush. Don't scrub the pot too hard, as you could damage the surface and bacteria might be introduced into the scratches, potentially harming your tree. You must also remove the mesh covering the drainage holes and replace it with fresh mesh and wire if required.

Step 3: Pruning the Roots

Pruning your tree's roots will help them get more nutrients from the soil. This will help your tree to remain healthy within its restricted environment. You want to keep as many of the newly formed fibrous feeder roots as possible and focus on cutting away the older and thicker storage roots. In order to safely do this, carefully comb out the old soil from the root mass with your chopstick or root hook. Starting from the base of the trunk and working outwards from the center toward the edges. This will free the roots and make it easier to see what is required for pruning.

You also want to ensure the feeder roots fit comfortably within the pot. Once the feeder roots reach the sides of the pot, they'll start growing in a circular pattern. This will end up restricting the amount of nutrients the tree will get. Also, remember that the longer the feeder roots are, the longer it will take for nutrients to reach the tree. A common practice of many enthusiasts is to try not to remove more than one-third of the root mass at any one time. This ensures you don't overly shock the tree.

Step 4: Returning the Tree to Its Pot

Once the roots are trimmed, you'll be able to return the tree to its pot. You'll start by adding a drainage layer to the bottom of the pot before adding the rest of the soil. We have a chapter dedicated to soil coming up, where we'll discuss the different types of soil that can be used for bonsai.

When adding the soil, remember to leave space for the tree's root system. You can do this by making a small mound of soil to rest your tree on before adjusting the roots. You need to make sure that you place your tree in the pot correctly. You may need to use wires to secure the roots and ensure the tree doesn't tip over. This is done by feeding the wires through the drainage holes and the sheet of mesh. Some pots are made with specific holes for wires. Having to readjust it after a few days will cause unnecessary stress to your tree and may affect its recovery time. As with branches, do not wire the roots too tightly to avoid restricting and damaging them as they grow.

When your tree is in the right position, you will fill the pot with soil and use a chopstick to remove any air pockets. You'll do this by gently poking the soil with the chopstick. This will ensure that the soil is touching the roots, enabling them to get all the nutrients they need from the soil.

The final step is to water your bonsai thoroughly. You might find that the water running out of the drainage holes is discolored. This will happen because of the new soil, so keep watering until the water running from the drainage holes is clear. You can then place your tree in a shaded spot for a few days while it recovers before returning it to its regular place.

Key Takeaways

- Bonsai trees need to be repotted to ensure that their roots still have enough space to absorb nutrients.

- The faster you want your tree to grow, the more often you'll want to repot it. More mature trees can be repotted less often.

- The best time to repot your tree is when it's coming out of its winter dormancy.

- Different types of pots will complement your tree's masculine or feminine characteristics.

- There are four steps to repotting your tree for optimal results.

Watering your bonsai tree will keep it healthy, but it isn't as simple as you may think. Many bonsai trees are lost due to incorrect watering practices. In the next chapter, we will give you all the knowledge you need to ensure you avoid making those same costly mistakes.

CHAPTER 6

WATER

Water is key to the survival of every living creature, including your bonsai tree. Successfully watering your tree may seem like a simple thing to master, but you would be surprised how many trees have been lost due to either over-watering or under-watering.

In this chapter, you'll learn some key techniques to keep your bonsai tree hydrated and healthy.

ABOUT CONTEMPORARY PHOTOGRAPHY

Watering Bonsai is an Art Form

Even though watering your bonsai tree isn't difficult, it's different from watering a regular houseplant. The restrictions made on the tree's roots mean it needs to be watered regularly, but because it's in a pot, the roots lose the ability to self-regulate how much water they absorb.

Every tree has different needs, so watering rules aren't cast in stone. If you purchase an already-established bonsai tree, you may receive in-depth care guidance from the vendor, but it's still important to get to know your tree, listen to it, and provide it with the attention it deserves.

How often you water your tree will depend on a number of factors, over and above your tree's species. You'll need to consider the season, humidity, and the type of soil your tree is planted in. In the summer, you'll probably need to water your tree more often than in the winter.

Let's take a look at the factors to consider before watering your tree in a little more detail.

Soil

Although we'll be discussing the optimum soil mixture for your bonsai in a later chapter, at this time, it's important to know that bonsai soil contains a variety of different components that are all designed to help the soil retain the maximum amount of moisture, while also being free draining. Different soil types can affect the required frequency of watering.

Fertilizer

Certain fertilizers can cause your bonsai soil to dry out faster, meaning that you'll have to water your tree more frequently.

Size of Your Tree

If you have a large tree or one that's growing very quickly, you may need to water it more regularly to ensure that it stays hydrated. Keep in mind that miniature bonsai trees might also need frequent watering, but the amount of water they're given will probably be less than what you'd give to a larger tree.

Pot Size

The bigger the pot, the more soil it can hold. The soil will help to retain the water, so it'll remain moist for longer. Just be mindful of tilting bigger pots from time to time to ensure water is distributed equally and drains efficiently.

Sunlight

Water evaporates in the heat of the sun, so how much sunlight your tree gets will help to determine how often you need water.

Weather Conditions

We have discussed the importance of keeping your bonsai protected from the elements. Not only can extreme weather conditions damage your tree, but strong winds can cause your tree's soil to dry out quickly. In the winter, freezing temperatures can cause the soil to freeze, making the absorption of water nearly impossible.

Checking Your Soil's Moisture Level

Regularly checking the soil's moisture level is the best way to determine if your tree needs water. Let's take a look at a few ways to check your soil.

Soil Moisture Meter

A soil moisture meter is arguably the most accurate way to check how moist your soil is. It's a great tool for beginners and experienced enthusiasts alike because it takes out any guesswork!

Different models of moisture meters might differ slightly, but they'll generally have a one to ten reading indicating a scale from dry to wet. To use a moisture meter, you'll simply insert the probe into the soil until it reaches your tree's roots. After a few seconds, you can make a note of the level that it shows. Be sure to clean the probe thoroughly before using it on another tree or putting it away.

If the reading is three or below, meaning the soil is slightly moist to dry, you need to water your tree.

The Chopstick Method

The chopstick method is an inexpensive way to check the soil's moisture. All you'll need is a wooden chopstick. You can even use a popsicle stick or any other wooden stick, as long as it's not painted or treated in any way.

Taking care not to damage any roots, you'll push the chopstick about 2 inches into the soil. This will depend on the size of your pot, so do take that into account. Ideally, you'll want to place the chopstick halfway between the tree and the edge of the pot.

Leave the chopstick in the soil for about 10 minutes. This will give the chopstick time to absorb moisture from the soil. After the 10 minutes have passed, take it out and examine it. If it's darker or has a solid watermark, the soil is perfect, and you don't need to water your tree.

If the chopstick has only slightly changed color, the soil is still moist, but you should check again the following day. If the chopstick hasn't changed color at all, the soil is completely dry, and you should water your tree.

Once you're done, you can wash the chopstick and leave it to dry. This method is great because you can check more than one tree's soil at a time. Just remember to have a dedicated chopstick for each tree!

When To Water Your Bonsai

When to water a bonsai tree is still a matter of debate among bonsai enthusiasts. The one thing that's agreed upon universally is to not water your bonsai tree during the hottest part of the day.

Ideally, you'll want to check on your tree early in the morning and late in the afternoon. If it needs to be watered in the morning, give your tree water. If you check again in the afternoon and it needs water again, by all means, water it again. This is especially true in the hot summer months.

It's important to remember that you can't put a bonsai tree on a watering schedule because there are too many factors that can affect its need for water. This is when you need to have a connection with your tree. You'll learn to listen to it and learn the signs it gives you when it needs water. Soon enough, you won't even need to check the soil's moisture. You'll just know.

Watering Methods

There are two widely used methods to water bonsai trees, so let's take a look at them now.

Top Watering

Top watering is when you pour a gentle stream of water over your tree, mimicking falling rain. The best way to achieve this is with a hose or watering can with a fine nozzle. You'll need to be careful not to wash away the top layer of soil, so keep your stream gentle. Be mindful during hot weather conditions to concentrate the water around the base of the tree and not directly on the leaves. This can lead to burnt leaves from the water evaporating too quickly in the heat and can be fatal to your tree.

If you see water gathering on the surface, give the soil a chance to soak it all in before continuing. When water starts leaking out of the drainage holes at the bottom of the pot, after a few seconds, you can stop watering. This indicates that the roots are watered sufficiently.

Immersion Watering

Immersion watering is like soaking your bonsai tree in a bath until it absorbs all the water it needs! Depending on the size of your pot, fill a tub or any other suitable container, with water and gently place the pot inside. The water in the tub should not spill into the pot itself. This is to prevent the soil from washing away during immersion. You can leave your pot in the tub for an hour or longer if necessary.

This method allows the soil to soak up water through the drainage holes at the bottom of the pot. Once the soil is sufficiently soaked, the soil simply won't absorb more water. When you remove the pot from the water, be sure to allow any excess to drain out.

If you're watering more than one bonsai tree, use separate tubs or containers to prevent cross-contamination.

Reviving a Struggling Bonsai Tree

Your bonsai tree might start showing signs that it is struggling, but that doesn't always mean that there's no way to revive it. Although daunting at first, you'll quickly be able to identify what your tree is struggling with, and you'll know what to do to nurse it back to health.

Over-watering can result in wilting, drooping, or discolored leaves. It is also a sign that root rot may be starting to set in. You'll need to reduce the amount of water you give your tree, allowing the soil to dry out completely before watering it again.

Under-watering your tree could also result in the same symptoms as well as the leaves turning yellow and dropping off very suddenly. The trunk and branches may also start shrinking. Make sure that there is enough soil in the pot, and ensure that you water it regularly. Adding more soil will give your tree's roots a greater area from which to absorb the water.

If root rot sets in, not only will your tree's leaves be discolored, but it will start giving off a slightly rotten smell. If you don't smell anything on the surface, try smelling the underside of the pot by the drainage holes. We will teach you how to deal with root rot and various tree health issues you may face in a later chapter.

How to Water Your Bonsai While You're Away

You're planning a family vacation, but your bonsai tree needs to be watered daily. What do you do? Fortunately, there are a few options if you aren't able to water your tree every day!

Firstly, you could ask a friend to come water your tree on a daily basis. Bonsai enthusiasts are sometimes reluctant to take this route because no one knows their bonsai tree quite like they do! So, let's take a look at a few alternatives.

Water Wicking

All you'll need to set up a water-wicking system is a container filled with water and some cotton rope or string. Carefully insert the string into your tree's soil, making sure that none of the roots are disturbed. You don't have to go too deep; an inch or two, depending on the size of the pot, is enough. Place the other end of the string in the container, making sure that it reaches the bottom.

This way, the string will provide a slow, steady, and constant supply of water to your tree.

Drip System

Another self-watering option is the drip system, and all you'll need is an empty plastic bottle and water.

Make a few holes in the bottle's lid and fill the bottle with water. Make a hole in the soil, making sure that none of the roots are disturbed, and insert the bottle lid first. As the soil dries out, water will be pulled into the soil from the bottle.

Immersion Watering

We discussed immersion watering earlier in this chapter, and it can be used to keep your bonsai tree watered if you're going away for a day or two. You might be thinking that root rot can develop, which is true, but it's not something that can happen overnight.

You may also use a bonsai drip tray underneath the pot. This is a quick alternative. Simply fill the tray with water and sit the bonsai pot on top. The water will be drawn up through the drainage holes. This method should only be used for a very short trip.

Temporary Greenhouse

You can create a temporary greenhouse for your bonsai tree by using a transparent plastic bag or container big enough to cover your tree. Make sure your tree is well watered, and then place the bag or container over the tree. You might need to inflate the bag a little to ensure that it's not touching the leaves. Place your temporary greenhouse in indirect sunlight. As the water evaporates from the soil, it will be trapped by the plastic bag and will drip back into the soil.

It's important to make sure that you don't place your temporary greenhouse in direct sunlight. This can cause the bag to heat up too much, damaging your tree.

Automated Watering Systems

An automated system uses a computer, piping, and valves to help regulate water flow. Some systems even allow you to install an app on your cell phone so that you can control when your tree is watered, regardless of your location. They can be purchased at gardening centers or online and will help to keep your tree watered while you're away.

The only downside to an automated system is that each bonsai tree has unique watering needs and this can't always be taken into account with this kind of system. This method can also prove to be very expensive.

Key Takeaways

- Each bonsai tree has unique watering needs.

- The conditions in which your tree lives need to be taken into consideration.

- It's important to check the moisture level in the soil.

- It's good practice to check moisture levels, and water, if necessary, twice a day.

- You can water your bonsai tree from the top, or you can immerse the pot in water.

- There are several ways in which you can keep your tree watered if you're unable to be there to do it yourself.

As you can see, watering a bonsai tree is similar, but also different, to watering a houseplant. With time, practice, and patience, you, too, will be an expert.

We've mentioned soil several times throughout this chapter; it's now time to get our hands dirty and dig deeper into the subject.

CHAPTER 7

SOIL

Soil choice is a hot topic among bonsai enthusiasts because there are so many different options available. In this chapter, we'll discuss what is available, from traditional mixes to modern, less expensive alternatives, all of which will give your tree the best benefits. There is no one soil mixture to rule them all; your personal preferences, budget, and location will determine your best course of action when it comes to soil selection.

Why Is Soil Important?

Because your bonsai tree is planted in a limited amount of soil, its importance can't be underestimated. Your tree needs to get all the nutrients and moisture it needs from this limited resource as opposed to its full-sized counterparts growing in the ground. It's important to ensure that the soil you're using is of great quality to give your tree everything it needs. So, what are the characteristics of good quality bonsai soil?

Water Retention

As discussed in our previous chapter, water is essential to the well-being of your tree, so the soil needs to be able to retain water effectively to be able to supply it with sufficient moisture.

Drainage

Although you need soil that retains water, it must also be able to provide sufficient drainage to release excess water and prevent root rot.

Aeration

The roots of your bonsai tree need air to absorb water and nutrients, so the soil mixture needs to leave tiny air pockets. This will also allow beneficial bacteria and fungi to break down nutrients for the roots to absorb. Pine trees, for example, need a healthy amount of a fungus called *Mycelium* in their soil to thrive.

Components of Bonsai Soil Mixes

Organic Components

Organic components consist of dead plant matter like peat, leaf litter, and bark. These compost mixtures are easily available at your local garden center. Because it's so easily available, many beginners start out using compost mixtures. It's great because it contains a lot of nutrients, and when it's fresh, it retains water very well.

There are a few drawbacks, though. As the plant matter decomposes, the soil's drainage can be compromised, increasing the possibility of health issues. The different types of plant matter also decompose at different speeds, so it's not always easy to know when the soil is no longer useful to your tree.

Organic components also tend to dry out very quickly and become compact. This will make watering your tree effectively a challenge due to its density. You'll see water running off the top of the soil and think your tree has had enough water, but in the meantime, none of the water has actually soaked through into the soil.

Inorganic Components

Inorganic components include volcanic lava, calcite, and baked clays. The lack of organic matter means that the mix has little nutritional value; however, they provide your tree with great drainage and aeration. Inorganic components don't always absorb as much water and nutrients, so it will allow you to control the amount of fertilizer in the soil more efficiently. It will also help with the development of finer roots.

Bonsai Soil Mixture Components

The most common bonsai soil mixtures are made up of several components, such as *akadama*, pumice, lava rock, and occasionally organic compost and gravel. Let's take a look at some of these components in a little more detail below.

Akadama

Akadama is a hard-baked Japanese clay that is specifically made for bonsai soil mixes and is available through online bonsai stores. It's great for drainage, water retention, and aeration. The large granules help with the drainage, but they're also porous, so they retain water. The granules do break down eventually, so it's important to check when repotting your tree; you may need to introduce fresh *akadama*.

Akadama is imported from Japan, which makes it quite expensive. However, you can use similarly fired clays, or some bonsai enthusiasts use cat litter as an effective, budget-friendly substitute. However, be careful to only use nonclumping brands of cat litter, as other types may well suffocate your tree's roots. Please use due diligence if considering this option.

Pumice

Pumice is a volcanic rock that is great at absorbing nutrients and water. It also provides support to growing roots.

Lava Rock

Like pumice, lava rock also helps to absorb water and provides growing roots with support. A mixture of all three of the previously mentioned components in equal measures is a very common and traditional bonsai soil mix that many commercial soil vendors will provide. As mentioned at the beginning of this chapter, soil mixtures can be varied and come down to personal preference. However, this traditional mix is a great starting point.

Organic Compost

As discussed earlier, organic compost is made up of dead plant matter, which is packed with nutrients. It retains water well but provides little drainage and aeration, especially when it dries out.

Gravel

Also known as grit, gravel can be added to help with drainage if required. Rougher gravel is sometimes layered at the bottom of the pot for this reason. It also can assist in keeping the soil aerated. Perlite, much like gravel, is another widely used substrate that provides great aeration and drainage.

Creating a Bonsai Soil Mixture

Using any of the components listed previously, you can create your own soil mixture for your tree. As you gain more experience with your tree, you can also adjust the mixture based on the conditions that your tree experiences. For example, if you live in a hot, dry area and you aren't able to check on your tree twice a day, you can add more absorbent substrate for additional water retention. If you live in a more humid climate, you can add more free-draining substrate.

Key Takeaways

- The correct soil mixture is important for drainage, water retention, and aeration.

- Bonsai soil mixes can be composed of organic and inorganic components.

- Organic components include dead plant matter, peat moss, and bark.

- Inorganic components include porous clay, volcanic rock, and gravel.

- Each tree needs its own mixture for optimal results. Be sure to research your tree's specific needs.

- You can adjust the quantities of certain components based on the conditions your tree experiences.

Because your tree's access to nutrients is limited, fertilizing is an essential part of bonsai care. In the next chapter, we'll be looking at how to fertilize your tree to help it grow and keep it healthy.

CHAPTER 8

FERTILIZER

We've already discussed how light, air, and water are essential for the health of your bonsai tree. Due to the restricted environment that your tree grows in, you'll need to supplement the nutrients in the soil with fertilizer. While there are a number of options available, some of which can be expensive, it's not always necessary to spend top dollar on a good fertilizer. In fact, it's even possible to create a great fertilizer for your tree from organic materials.

The Main Components in Fertilizer

When you start looking at fertilizers at your local garden center, you may be overwhelmed by all the options available to you. Which will be the best for your tree? Let's take a look at the three main components found in common fertilizers, namely nitrogen, potassium, and phosphorus.

Nitrogen (N)

Nitrogen is essential for the development of strong branches and leaves. It helps trees to form protein, which is essential for all above-ground growth. In nature, trees can get nitrogen from the soil, as well as from rain. Nitrogen is the most important element for all bonsai trees.

Potassium (K)

Another important element for bonsai trees is potassium. It encourages optimal sap flow in your tree's trunk and branches, and it helps your tree resist infection. Potassium also helps your tree deal with stress by activating enzymes in the cells.

Phosphorus (P)

Phosphorus helps your tree create energy and encourages healthy root, fruit, and flower growth.

Other Elements

While the three previously mentioned elements are the main macronutrients you'll find in fertilizer, you will also find iron, manganese, zinc, and copper, among others.

When browsing fertilizers at your garden center, you'll notice a series of three numbers on each bag, for example, 10-10-10. These numbers are the percentages of nitrogen, potassium, and phosphorus in the fertilizer mix. This is also known as the N-P-K value.

Which Fertilizer to Choose?

Outdoor bonsai need a higher nitrogen content, so an N-P-K of 10-6-6 is highly recommended in the spring. During the summer, the nitrogen content can be in balance with the potassium and phosphorus content, so an N-P-K of 6-6-6 works great. In the autumn, you'll want to drop the nitrogen even further to an N-P-K of 3-6-6. These are not hard and fast rules but basic guidelines to consider when choosing your fertilizer during the changing seasons.

Of course, your tree's development stage is an important factor to consider. Young bonsai trees need to grow rapidly, so a stronger fertilizer is needed. In the meantime, a fully matured tree will need fertilizer aimed at maintaining its health.

Types of Fertilizers

Fertilizers come in liquid and solid forms, each of which has its own advantages and disadvantages. You will also find organic and synthetic varieties, so let's take a closer look at them here.

Liquid Fertilizer

Liquid fertilizers are a great way to introduce nutrients to the soil quickly. However, the nutrients are lost when watering, and during heavy downpours of rain, so a regular fertilizing schedule is needed.

Solid Fertilizer

Solid fertilizers are spread on the surface of the soil. When you water your tree, the granules start to dissolve, and in doing so, nutrients are slowly introduced into the soil. The slow release of nutrients means you won't need to fertilize your tree as often. The drawback is that the granules can damage your tree's roots, and it's not always easy to know when to add more fertilizer.

Organic Fertilizer

Organic fertilizers are created using organic matter such as seaweed, manure, and other plant matter. Seaweed is a relatively new addition to organic fertilizer in the Western world, although it's been used in China since 2700 B.C.E. It has been found that seaweed improves plant growth, protein, and carbohydrate production, and increases levels of photosynthesis.

The upside is that the elements are released slowly, and there is no risk of damaging your tree's roots. Unfortunately, organic fertilizers don't always have the micronutrients that your tree needs, and due to the matter that makes up organic fertilizers, they can have a strong smell.

Synthetic Fertilizer

Synthetic fertilizers are created in laboratories and take into account the ratio of not just the macronutrients that each tree species needs but also the micronutrients. The nutrients are released quickly and can be slow-releasing, meaning you won't need to fertilize as often.

They can, however, cause a chemical build-up in the soil, which is harmful to your tree. Synthetic fertilizers also run the risk of burning your tree's roots if applied incorrectly. The trick is to follow the instructions on the package for the best results.

When to Fertilize Your Bonsai Tree

The best time to fertilize your outdoor bonsai tree is during its peak growing season, beginning in the early spring until approximately mid-autumn. This is when your tree will need the most nutrients to produce new stems, leaves, flowers, and fruit. Indoor bonsai trees can be fertilized year-round.

Young trees need to be fertilized on a weekly basis because they're growing fast and need plenty of nutrients to do so. As your tree matures, you can cut back on the fertilizing schedule. By the time your tree is fully matured, you may be able to fertilize it once per month.

Each category of tree does have its own specific schedule that you should follow to ensure the optimal health of your tree. We highly recommend that you spend some time researching your tree's specific requirements.

Tropical Bonsai

Tropical bonsai trees can be fertilized weekly from the beginning of spring to the end of autumn. Although you can still fertilize them in the winter, it's important to remember that their growth does slow down. If you see this happening, you can reduce your fertilization schedule to every third or fourth week.

Coniferous Bonsai

Coniferous bonsai can be fertilized weekly between spring and autumn. In the winter, you can fertilize them once a month, and you should also use less fertilizer than in the warmer months. Just be aware that coniferous trees, such as pines, tend to grow more slowly.

Deciduous Bonsai

A good rule of thumb is to aim to fertilize deciduous bonsai every second week between spring and autumn. Some bonsai enthusiasts don't fertilize their deciduous bonsai during the winter, while others use nitrogen-free fertilizer.

Things to Remember When Fertilizing Your Bonsai Tree

A tree that's suffered stress won't respond well to fertilizer as it will often shock its system even more. If your tree is sick, if it's just been repotted, or if it's dehydrated, don't fertilize it. Wait at least one month for the tree to recover before reintroducing fertilizers.

Remember to read the instructions on your fertilizer's packaging to ensure that you're using the right amount of fertilizer on your tree. Over-fertilizing can harm your tree's roots. Other symptoms of over-fertilizing include discolored or dying leaves, fertilizer residue on top of the soil, and slowed growth.

If you suspect you've over-fertilized your tree, rinse the soil by thoroughly watering it and trimming away any damaged leaves or branches. Leave your tree to recover for one month before introducing fertilizer again.

Key Takeaways

- Nitrogen, potassium, and phosphorus are key elements needed by bonsai trees.

- The N-P-K value on fertilizer indicates the percentages of nitrogen, potassium, and phosphorus.

- Fertilizers can be liquid, solid, organic, and synthetic.

- Most bonsai trees need regular fertilizing from spring to autumn.

- Don't fertilize sick or stressed trees.

Although fertilizing a bonsai tree can seem like a daunting task for a beginner, please be reassured that by following the guidance in this chapter and carefully reading the instructions on your chosen fertilizer, you will soon get the hang of it. If you are still feeling unsure, then perhaps you may want to consider joining your local bonsai club or online forum. We'll discuss this more in a later chapter.

Now for the fun part! Styling your tree.

CHAPTER 9

SHAPING AND STYLING

Shaping and styling your bonsai tree is where you can get creative and have fun! After carefully looking after your tree and ensuring that it's healthy, you'll be able to start training it into your desired shape.

Advanced Bonsai Shapes and Styles

In Chapter 3, we looked at four of the most popular bonsai shapes and styles for beginners, namely, the formal and informal upright styles, as well as the slanting and cascading styles.

As your expertise grows, you can start experimenting with more advanced styles like the ones listed below.

Broom-Style Bonsai

The *Hokidachi*, or broom-style, is best suited to deciduous trees that have plenty of fine branches. The trunk stands upright, and the branches fan out, making up approximately one-third of the tree's height. The branches and leaves are kept in a ball shape, which thins out in the cooler months.

Semi-Cascading Bonsai Style

The *Han-kengai*, or semi-cascading style, is similar to the cascading style, but the trunk and branches never grow below the bottom of the pot. In nature, trees growing along riverbanks are shaped like this.

Wind-Swept Bonsai Style

The *Fukinagashi*, or wind-swept style, is another example of a tree that has grown in extremely windy conditions. The trunk isn't straight like in the slanting style but is allowed to be slightly crooked. It must still grow predominantly in a curved, slanted direction. The branches and leaves only grow on the side to which the trunk is curving.

Literati Bonsai Style

The *Bunjingi*, or literati style, can be observed in nature when trees have to compete with each other for light, meaning that they have to grow taller than the trees that surround them. The trunk tends to grow crooked, lacking branches, until the crown, as this is the only area that gets enough direct sunlight on the branches and leaves. When styling a bonsai in this manner, enthusiasts tend to create a Jin in places along the trunk line. This means that the bark is removed leaving the exposed bare wood of a branch. A large section of trunk without bark is known as Shari.

Double-Trunk Bonsai Style

The *Sokan*, or double-trunk style, may be common in nature but less so in bonsai. Both trunks can grow out of the ground, but you can also have a secondary, thinner trunk growing from the main trunk just above ground level. The main trunk tends to grow upright, while the secondary trunk is slightly slanted. Both trunks can have plenty of branches and leaves.

Multi-Trunk Bonsai Style

The *Kabudachi*, or multi-trunk style, is similar to the double-trunk style but needs to have at least three trunks. Each trunk will develop its own branches and leaves, but the one from the main trunk must be the fullest and thickest.

Forest Bonsai Style

The *Yose-ue*, or forest style, may look similar to the multi-trunk style, but it consists of multiple trees instead of one tree with many trunks. The most developed trees are planted in the center of the pot, with the smaller trees around them. The trees are planted in a staggered pattern to more closely resemble the growth of trees in a natural forest.

Root Over Rock Bonsai Style

The *Seki-joju*, or on a rock style, resembles trees in nature that grow on mountains and have to extend their root systems over rocks to find nutrients in the soil found in nooks and crannies. The roots grow a special type of bark to protect them from the sun.

Techniques for Styling and Shaping Your Tree

The two main techniques used for styling and shaping your tree are pruning and wiring. Both these techniques will be discussed in more detail in the following chapters, so we will just look at the overview here.

Pruning

Pruning is the removal of parts of the tree, like branches or buds, to ensure that growth takes place in the desired direction. Depending on the type of tree and how mature it is, you could prune it two or three times per year.

Wiring

Wiring is the process of winding wire around the trunk or branches to ensure that they grow in a certain direction. After months, or even years, the wire can be removed, and the branch will stay in place.

How to Decide on a Style

Deciding on a style or shape for your bonsai tree is a very personal decision, but you will need to take your tree into consideration. Remember, the objective of bonsai is to emulate a full-grown tree in miniature, so it's always a good idea to start off by looking at how your tree's full-grown counterpart grows.

Look at your tree from all sides and find the best starting point for your desired style. Most bonsai trees have a distinct front and back, so it may help you to mark the front of your tree to remind you of where you'll be concentrating your efforts.

Also, take your tree's branches into consideration. The more branch growth your tree has, the more style options you'll have available. If you have too many branches for your desired style, you can always cut them back. Remember, you can start out with a few desired styles, and as you work on your tree, you'll be able to narrow it down to the one style that's most suitable for it.

Key Takeaways

- Deciding on a style and shape is a personal choice. There is no right or wrong style.

- Pruning and wiring are the two main techniques for styling and shaping your bonsai tree.

- When deciding on a style, look at how your tree's full-grown counterpart grows in nature.

In the next two chapters, we'll be discussing pruning and wiring your tree to create your desired style.

CHAPTER 10

PRUNING

As your bonsai tree grows, you'll need to prune it to make sure that it grows into your desired style. It may be daunting to start cutting off branches and twigs after watching your tree grow, but it helps your tree stay healthy and look beautiful.

During the growing season, trees will produce new branches and growth that may be unwanted or that impact the overall design of the bonsai. Pruning is a key skill to learn to shape and keep unwanted growth in check.

Understanding How Trees Grow

Before you start pruning, it's important to understand how trees grow. This foundational knowledge will give you an advantage when pruning your tree.

You'll see that any branches growing from your tree's trunk are thicker and more dominant than any smaller branches and twigs growing from those main branches. This allows trees to grow taller, especially when competing for light with the trees that surround them. As the tree grows taller and develops branches higher up along the trunk, the lower branches tend to die off. In bonsai, this isn't always the effect that you want.

The way that you prune your tree affects the way that it will grow. For example, if you want a taller tree, you'll prune the lower branches. But if you want your tree to develop stronger branches lower down the trunk, you'll need to prune the top of your tree. This is how you'll be able to control your tree's growth, overall height, and style.

Why Prune?

There are two main reasons why you'll need to prune your tree. The first is for maintenance, to ensure that your tree maintains its shape. The second is structural pruning, which is a lot more intensive, as you'll be creating the shape you want for your tree.

Maintenance Pruning

The main aim of maintenance pruning is to make sure that your tree's shape and style are maintained and perfected. Because your tree will mostly grow upwards, you'll find that you will have to concentrate the majority of your pruning on the higher canopy to ensure that the lower branches grow stronger.

Bonsai trees can be pruned year-round, although the best time is during the growing season, from early spring to late autumn.

When pruning your tree for maintenance, you'll focus on the areas where your tree is outgrowing the desired shape. Think of maintenance pruning as giving your tree a haircut, trimming off any scraggly bits that make its shape look messy.

When pruning, you need to use twig cutters or regular shears for the best results. Using the correct tools when pruning your tree will drastically reduce the stress caused to it. With pine trees and a few other species of conifer, it's best to pinch off any unwanted foliage or branches with your fingers. Using shears will lead to dead foliage where the cut was made. Some species of trees will need a combination of pruning with shears and pruning by pinching, so it's best to read up on your species to avoid mishaps. Juniper is a commonly styled tree that requires both techniques.

A third method of pruning your tree is called defoliation. This involves pruning the leaves of the tree as opposed to the twigs or branches of deciduous or broadleaf evergreen trees. This can only be done during the summer months, and it will force your tree to grow new leaves. The objective behind this method is to aid your tree in growing new, smaller leaves that are in proportion to your tree's height, as well as to increase ramification.

Structural Pruning

Structural pruning is when you're working on giving your tree the shape you've chosen. It can be a challenge because you'll be cutting off thicker branches to achieve the desired result. Cutting off branches is irreversible and will define the shape of your tree, so you should be certain of what style you're aiming toward. Keeping that in mind, you should also remember that the different styles aren't set in stone, so you can make these decisions based on your own intuition. Who knows? Maybe you'll discover a new shape for bonsai trees!

The best time to prune your tree for structure is either before or after the growing season, so very early spring or late autumn. Of course, the exact timing will be different for each species, so it's best to check what's best for your tree.

To prune your tree, you should examine it at eye level to help you determine which branches should stay and which should go. The trunk of your tree is an important feature, and it needs to be clear of any obstructions. Take it slow, but a good starting point would be to look at the first pair of lowest branches and work upwards from there.

Here are a few other branches you may wish to remove that could affect the overall composition of your tree.

- Branches that crisscross over each other.

- Branches growing vertically.

- Any branches that obstruct the view of branches you want to keep.

- Branches growing back toward the trunk.

- Branches with twists and turns.

- Branches growing outside the tree's profile.

- Thick branches near the top of the tree.

- Branches growing on the opposite sides of the trunk at the same height, these are commonly known as bar branches.

- Branches that are growing toward your chosen front, blocking the tree's trunkline.

Concave cutters are the tool of choice for pruning large branches. Using regular shears can leave an unsightly scar where the cut was made. When making these large cuts, it's best to use wound sealant to protect your tree from infection and to speed up the healing process.

It's important to remember that your tree needs time to recover from structural pruning. You shouldn't do any additional work on your bonsai for one full year after a structural pruning session.

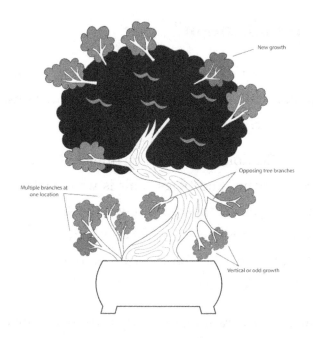

New growth

Opposing tree branches

Multiple branches at one location

Vertical or odd growth

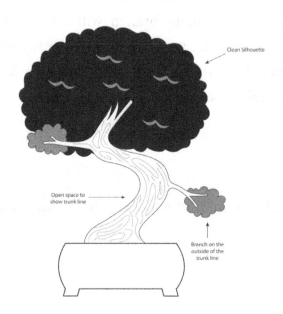

Clean Silhouette

Open space to show trunk line

Branch on the outside of the trunk line

What Is Ramification?

Ramification is the process of growing, pruning, cutting, and dividing primary and secondary branches on your bonsai tree to make it look fuller.

In nature, ramification happens when branches and stems divide into smaller branches and twigs. This is what makes trees look full and lush. In bonsai, the aim is to get the same look by pruning and training your tree to grow smaller branches and twigs. Remember, you want your bonsai tree to look like a miniature replica of a full-grown tree.

You can observe low ramification when there is only one small branch extending out from a larger branch. In contrast, with high ramification, a main branch will have multiple smaller branches growing from it, and those smaller branches will have twigs growing from them. These twigs will grow leaves and give your tree its full appearance.

Let's look at examples of good and bad ramification in bonsai trees.

In the image above, you'll see an example of good ramification. The tree has plenty of branches originating from the trunk. The branches also have smaller branches and twigs growing, and these are usually kept in place by wiring, which we'll discuss in the following chapter.

This has resulted in a tree with full foliage replicating its full-grown counterpart.

Bad bonsai ramification can look something like the image above, where the tree doesn't have many branches and stems. The few branches that are growing from the trunk will need time to develop and grow smaller branches and twigs. Just a quick disclaimer: the second image is of a Ficus bonsai, and the lack of ramification is due to its species. We've used this image merely as an example.

To improve the ramification, you would need to trim some of the longer branches at their nodes to help the tree develop more branches. Nodes are the points on a tree's branch where the leaf buds appear. The internode is the distance between two nodes. A good example of a tree with long internodes is the maple. Trimming and pruning these annually will shorten the distance between nodes increasing leaf density and ramification, giving the much-desired fuller look.

Good ramification not only makes your tree look like its full-grown counterpart, but it also gives you a good foundation to work with when you start shaping your tree. It's always better to have too much to work with as opposed to not enough.

To increase the ramification of your tree, you'll need to prune mature branches with concave shears just after the nodes of the branch. When it starts growing again, new branches will form from the nodes, resulting in more branches, twigs, and leaves. It's important only to prune branches that are fully matured, as younger branches might not sprout new growth. If you're interested in trees with naturally great ramification, consider purchasing a Chinese elm.

Healing Wounds

Pruning your tree will inevitably leave wounds on the trunk and branches. If not treated properly, they can leave unsightly scarring, which will aesthetically damage your tree's style. While merely giving your tree time to heal will help, there are other methods that can be used to ensure that any scarring is minimal.

Let's look at a few things to consider regarding wounds both before and after you prune your tree.

Before You Prune

- **Wound size**

  If you're able to minimize the size of the wound, you're already halfway there! The smaller the wound you make on your tree, the quicker it will heal and the smaller the scar will be. Sometimes it's better to make a number of small cuts on your tree, spread out over time, to achieve the style you want than making one large cut. Of course, it's easy to think that making more cuts will cause more stress on your tree and create more scars, but as you know, the smaller cuts will heal faster. Think of a paper cut on your finger versus the damage a knife can do. Try to keep your cuts on the small side where possible.

- **The size and age of your tree**

  The one advantage that you'll have with younger trees is that they're still growing, so it's likely that the wound will have time to heal and that it'll be covered by newer bark as your tree develops. Older and larger trees will take longer to heal.

- **Leaving a stub**

  To minimize the wounds and scars on your tree's trunk, you can always leave a stub when you prune. This means that you don't remove the whole branch or twig, but you leave a little behind. This method will reduce the amount of damage to the tree. When you leave a stub, the trunk or main branch builds a barrier so that nutrients aren't delivered to the stub, leaving it to die back. The barrier also stops bacteria and viruses from making their way into the tree. You can then prune the dead stubs away the following year.

- **Your tools**

  To minimize the size of the wound on your tree, you need to ensure that your tools are sharp. Clean tools will also ensure that no bacteria, viruses, or fungi are introduced to your tree during a pruning session.

After You Prune

- **Time to recover**

  The best way to promote healing is to give your tree time to grow and recover. Make sure your tree gets the water, light, and nutrients it needs so that it's able to heal the wound and grow around it.

- **Wound sealant**

  Many bonsai enthusiasts prefer using wound sealant after a pruning session. It protects the tree from bacteria and viruses trying to get in and helps to keep moisture and nutrients in the tree. You'll find a variety of wound sealants, like paste, silver stickers, or even regular wood glue. The paste is the most common variety and the one we would recommend above all others. After pruning, you'll dab some paste on the wound and leave it there to harden.

Key Takeaways

- Pruning is done for maintenance and to create structure.

- The best time to do structural pruning is either before or after its growing season, so early spring or late autumn.

- Ensure that your pruning tools are sharp and clean.

- You can take a number of steps to ensure that your tree heals quickly after a pruning session.

- Your tree will need time to recover, so allow it to rest for at least one year after a structural pruning session.

- It is advisable to avoid structural pruning and root pruning at the same time, as this can have a detrimental effect on your tree.

In the next chapter, we'll be discussing wiring techniques that are used to train the branches of your tree to grow in a specific direction, resulting in your desired style.

CHAPTER 11

WIRING

Wiring is a convenient and easy way to train your tree's branches to grow in the direction most suitable for your desired shape. Many beginners tend to be wary of wiring, believing that the wire will bite into the branches or that they might snap the branches when trying to place the wires.

In this chapter, you'll discover the fundamentals of wiring, why it's beneficial, and how to do it correctly.

Types of Wire

Before we dive into how to wire your tree, let's look at the different types of wire that you can use.

Aluminum Wire

Aluminum wire is soft and very easy to use. It bends easily, so if you make a mistake, it's simple to correct it. The wire is usually anodized, meaning that it's been treated to be corrosion-resistant, and is usually black or brown in color, allowing it to be easily camouflaged on your tree's branches. Rest assured that the anodizing process won't change the properties of the aluminum and is perfectly safe for your tree.

The advantage of aluminum wire is that it is less likely to damage your tree's bark. The downside, however, is that the branches you've wired may return to their original shape and direction due to the wire's flexibility.

Choosing the correct thickness of wire is crucial for successful wiring. If the wire is too thick, it can damage your tree. If it's too thin, the wired branches won't stay in place. The wire shouldn't be thicker than the branch you're going to use it on. A good guide is to use wire that's approximately two-thirds of the branch's girth.

To test if your wire is the right thickness, take a length of wire and place it in your hand, making sure that a few inches are unsupported by your hand. Press the unsupported part of the wire against the branch that needs to be wired. If the wire bends, it's too thin. If the branch bends, then you've got the right thickness.

Copper Wire

For copper wire to be used on a bonsai tree, it needs to go through the annealing process. During this process, the copper is heated up to help soften it. Regular earthing copper wire from your local hardware store hasn't gone through this process, so it'll be too hard for your tree.

Copper wire is much stronger than aluminum wire, so it'll retain its shape for much longer and will hold your tree's branches in place. Unfortunately, its strength means it's difficult to straighten after it's been used, so it won't be possible to reuse old wire. The advantage is that you'll need to use a lot less of it due to its strength.

Because copper wire is much stronger than aluminum, you can use wire that is half the thickness of what you would've used if it were aluminum.

Wiring Your Tree

When to Wire

Although there is no set guideline, the best time to wire your tree is during its growing season. Wiring your tree's branches can cause small cracks, and they will heal faster in the growing season. Let's see when the best time is to wire your tree.

Outdoor Deciduous Trees

Early spring is the best time to wire outdoor deciduous trees. The lack of leaves will give you a clear view of the branches that need to be wired, and there will be no risk of damaging new leaves. It's important to be aware of the tree's new buds so that they aren't broken off or damaged during the wiring process. As the tree enters the growing season, the new shape will solidify quickly. You'll have to keep an eye on the tree as the branches grow. The wire will become tighter, and if left unchecked, it will begin to bite into the branches. Removing wire that's embedded into the bark will leave unsightly scars on your tree. This can spoil the aesthetics of your tree and is not easy to remedy, so take care and check your trees regularly.

Summer is another good time to wire your outdoor deciduous tree. Although the leaves may obstruct your view, you'll be able to leave the wire in place for longer because the growth has slowed down. However, the growth is still fast enough to have the branches set in place relatively quickly.

Wiring can also take place in autumn, and the wires can remain in place until the following year. Your tree's growth will have slowed down drastically, and the falling leaves will once again give you a good view of the branches that need work.

It's not recommended to wire an outdoor deciduous tree in the winter months. Bending the branches can cause cracks, and because the tree is dormant, these won't heal well, resulting in unsightly scars and increasing the risk of infection.

Indoor Tropical and Subtropical Trees

For the majority of indoor tropical or subtropical trees, you may wire any time of year. The only requisite is that they get enough light and warmth throughout the year, which encourages the growing and healing process. If your tree is showing any signs of ill health, don't wire it.

Evergreen Coniferous Trees

Your evergreen coniferous tree can be wired from spring to early autumn. Because they tend to be slower growers, the wire will usually need to stay on for a longer period. Just as with deciduous trees, it's important to check the wire regularly to ensure that it's not biting into the branch.

If you need to keep the wire on the tree during the winter months, make sure that it's placed in a frost-free area. Sheltering is a key part of protecting your trees during colder periods, and we will go into more detail about this topic later in the book.

Where to Wire

When you're deciding where to wire your tree, you need to keep the style you want in mind. This will help you to decide if you need to wire the whole tree or just a few select branches.

Applying the Wire

If you need to wire your tree's trunk, you'll need to anchor the wire in the soil. Simply insert the wire two to three inches into the soil until it feels stable. You can then start to coil the wire from the base of the trunk, moving up and around roughly at a 45-degree angle per coil.

When you're wiring branches, you'll need to anchor the wire to the trunk itself. Again, you'll wrap the wire around the trunk before wiring the branch, working from the trunk outwards. This is known as single-wiring.

Double-wiring is when you wire two pieces of smaller-sized wire together. This creates a much thicker and stronger wire out of the two thinner pieces. This is good for when you are low on varying thicknesses of wire and need additional support.

The Two-Branch Principle

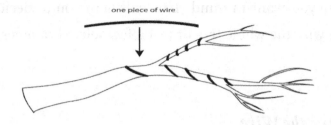

The two-branch principle is regarded as the best way to wire two branches with one piece of wire. This not only saves time but will also result in you using less wire per tree, saving you money in the long run.

This method can also be used to wire opposing branches on opposite sides of the main trunk by just using one wire.

Wiring in this way provides great stability and allows for safer bends to be created. The way to do this with one piece of wire is to visualize the two branches you wish to work on and measure out a piece of wire that, once folded in half, will wrap around both branches. This isn't something you can just measure with a ruler, this is more to do with feel, but you will become better with practice. It is better to overestimate the size of the wire than to come up short.

Once you have your piece of wire ready, gently bend the wire in half. Place the newly formed bend on the area where the branches intersect before splitting off. Coiling one branch first following the same techniques as above. Once the first branch is wired, it will be easier to then wire the second branch with the remaining section of wire. Once in place, those two branches can now be manipulated into your desired position.

When wiring two opposing branches, follow the same technique, but this time, you will not need to bend the wire in half, but you will still place the center of the wire on the halfway point between those branches, which will normally be in line with the main trunk.

It's also important to make sure that each wrap around the trunk or branch is consistent in its spacing. Make sure that your wires don't cross over each other at any point. This will damage the bark and leave an unsightly scar.

Once the wire is in place, you can start positioning the branches. It's recommended that you lightly push the branches into the desired position, so for example, if you want the branch to move down, you'll support the bottom of the branch and slowly push it from the top down. Be careful at this stage and take your time.

Another method used to shape branches is to wire the end section of a branch with a long piece of wire and then secure this to the base or sides of the pot. The wire is then put under tension until the branch is moved downwards into the desired position, similar to using guy ropes on a tent.

A common mistake with any of these techniques is to rush the process, which will only result in snapped branches. This can ruin your overall design and can set you back many years.

Rest and Recovery

After applying the wire, put your tree in a shady spot with plenty of indirect light. You can water and fertilize your tree normally. It's important to keep an eye on the wires to make sure that they're not digging into the bark, especially with deciduous trees.

Removing the Wire

The wire needs to stay on the tree for as long as possible to make sure that the branch or trunk stays in the position you want, but not so long that it starts damaging your tree. This could take a few weeks or even months!

The best time to remove the wire is when it starts getting tighter around the branch, but before it really starts digging into the bark.

You'll need to establish a regular routine to check the wiring on your tree and keep track of how fast it's growing. The speed at which it grows depends on the species of tree, the time of year, and how much fertilizer you've been giving your tree.

You'll notice that some branches might grow quicker than others, so you'll need to remove the wire there first. Just because you wired everything that you needed to wire at the same time doesn't mean you need to remove all the wire at the same time too. Keep checking up on the wires to determine which need to be removed and which need to stay on a little longer. As long as the wire isn't damaging your tree, the wires can stay on.

We discussed the benefits of purchasing wire cutters in the tool section. Not only do they make the job easier to remove the wire, but they also help to protect the branches when removing the wire. If you don't have any wire cutters, you can try to unravel the wire by hand. Please be careful because this is where you could break the branch in a similar fashion to setting the wire. It may be easier to remove aluminum wire than copper by hand. Removing wire by hand can be cost-effective because you can then use the wire again, but as we've previously mentioned, it's much safer for your tree to cut the wire in small sections to remove it. We believe it's better to lose a cheaper piece of wire than an expensive branch.

Key Takeaways

- Wiring your bonsai tree will help you set and achieve your desired shape or style.

- You can use aluminum or copper wire.

- The thickness of the wire you use depends on the thickness of the branch you want to wire.

- Depending on your tree's species and where it's placed, you can wire your tree throughout the year.

- You can wire your tree's trunks and branches using the different methods discussed.

- After the wire is applied, keep checking on your tree to make sure that it isn't biting into the bark.

- You don't have to remove all the wires at the same time.

In the next chapter, we'll be looking at a hot topic in bonsai circles: What techniques can you use to get a thicker trunk?

CHAPTER 12

POT VS. GROUND

Most beginners will want to kick off their bonsai journey with an already-established tree, but this might be an expensive way to start. Finding a young tree in a nursery or garden center is a much less costly way to get started. You can also search for and collect trees growing in nature that can easily be dug up and replanted in a pot. This is known as *yamadori*, and you will be delighted to know that we have a full chapter dedicated to this later in the book.

Starting off with young material will be cheaper, but it'll take longer for your tree to grow thick roots and branches. To speed up the process, you can plant your tree in the ground first before transplanting it into a bonsai pot.

Planting in the Ground

Benefits

A tree will develop much faster when planted in the ground because it has an unlimited supply of water and nutrients. This will allow its roots to develop outside the constraints of the bonsai pot. Planting in the ground will also help to prevent root rot because excess water is spread out throughout the soil in your yard.

If your potted tree is struggling and the trunk isn't as thick as you'd like, planting it in the ground will give it the freedom to spread out its roots, access more nutrients and experience an increased rate of growth.

It's also a much more cost-effective way to keep a bonsai tree. You won't need to fertilize a tree planted in the ground as often because it will get the majority of the nutrients it needs from the soil.

Drawbacks

A few things that discourage gardeners from planting their bonsai trees in the ground is that they'll be more susceptible to pests and damage.

Many gardeners become bonsai enthusiasts because they don't have the space to have a full-grown tree in their yards. You may live in an apartment with no garden, so planting your tree in the ground is simply not an option.

Planting in a Pot

Benefits

Bonsai enthusiasts love the convenience of having their trees in a bonsai pot and the aesthetic it brings to their gardens and workspace.

Having your tree indoors also gives you a lot more control over the environment. You can make sure it gets enough, but not too much water, sunlight, and nutrients. While the risk of pests is still there, it will be a lot less due to the controlled environment.

Drawbacks

Keeping your bonsai in a pot means that you'll have to spend more time ensuring that it gets all the water and nutrients that it needs. Your tree will also be more prone to root issues because of the confines of the pot.

Of course, the tree's growth will be limited to the size of the pot in which it's planted due to the limitations of its growing space.

Root and Trunk Development

Many bonsai enthusiasts will plant saplings in the ground for a few years as this allows for rapid root growth. Rapid root growth, in turn, helps the trunk to grow faster. After a few years, the tree is then replanted in the bonsai pot.

Many of the pots used in bonsai are shallow and elongated, meaning that lateral root growth is encouraged. But how can you promote lateral root growth when your tree is planted in the ground?

A trick that's used in bonsai circles is to bury a tile or slab under the tree's root mass. This will limit the growth of the tap root and will promote the growth of lateral roots.

Replanting Into a Pot

Once your tree's trunk is thick enough, you need to replant your tree into its pot so that it doesn't grow into a full-sized tree. This can be a daunting experience, even for the more experienced gardener, but there are a few things to keep in mind to help you replant your tree successfully. The best time to do this is in the very early spring before the tree goes into its growth cycle. However, pines are an exception to this rule as they tend to be better transferred into a pot in early autumn.

First, you need to dig around the tree, aiming to disturb the lateral roots as little as possible. Keep some of the soil from the ground to use in your potting mixture. Place your tree on damp sheets so that it retains as much moisture as possible. Trim the tap root if necessary, using your root cutters.

Ensure you select a pot that is big enough to accommodate your tree. This will give it the space to grow more in the future. Add the soil from the ground your tree was planted in to ensure the fibrous roots aren't shocked by the sudden change of environment. Make sure your tree is stable, and fresh soil is added and packed well.

Using a fine nozzle, water your tree until the water from the drainage holes runs clear. You can place the pot outdoors, protected from direct sunlight, so that it can recuperate. Leave your tree to recuperate for at least one year before you repot it or begin styling it. During its first summer in the pot, you can introduce small quantities of fertilizer.

Key Takeaways

- Planting your tree in the ground for a few years will help its roots and trunk to grow faster and thicker.

- Once the desired trunk size is achieved, it can be replanted in a pot.

- Leave your tree to recuperate for at least one year.

Regardless of whether you plant your tree in the ground or in a bonsai pot, you will still be faced with the same issues of keeping your tree healthy and pest-free. Even the greatest bonsai masters are not immune to these challenges. In our next chapter, we will cover the common pests and health issues you might face throughout your bonsai journey.

CHAPTER 13

PESTS AND DISEASES

Whencomes to pest control, prevention is better than the cure. Examining your tree for pests on a regular basis and taking the necessary steps to prevent them will greatly improve your tree's health and longevity.

In this chapter, you'll discover the most common pests and diseases that bonsai trees are susceptible to, as well as how to treat an infested or infected tree.

Signs of a Diseased or Infested Tree

Despite your best efforts, your tree can become infested with pests or be infected with a disease. Spotting the signs of disease or infestation early on will make the treatment faster and recuperation time quicker.

Here are the signs that your tree is infected with disease or infested with pests:

- discolored leaves or flowers

- out-of-season loss of leaves

- yellow, wilted, or dried leaves

- slow growth

- dieback—leaves and shoots that start dying from the tip

Common Pests

Being able to identify the pest or disease on your tree quickly will give you the upper hand in treating your tree. Listed below are some of the most common pests and health issues you may battle against. Be aware that your location on the world map will dictate the kinds of pests and health issues you are likely to face. We would highly recommend that you learn as much as possible about your local environment and its unique biodiversity. Seeking out a knowledgeable, green-fingered friend or local bonsai group would be an advisable course of action.

Aphids

Aphids are tiny insects that suck the sap from your tree. They can usually be found in clusters under your tree's leaves, secreting a sugary substance that ants and mold feed on. They can also introduce diseases to your tree.

If your tree has aphids, you may see deformed shoots and weak leaves and branches.

Red Spider Mites

Red spider mites are almost invisible and can cause significant damage to your tree. They prefer a warm, dry climate. If your tree is infested with spider mites, the leaves will start yellowing before turning brown. Coniferous trees are most susceptible to spider mites.

Scale Insects

If your tree is infested with scale insects, the bark of your tree will have white, yellow, or brown bumps on it. The branches will start drooping, and the leaves will turn yellow and drop off. Scale insects suck sap from the tree and are usually found in clusters.

Caterpillars

Caterpillars can quickly destroy a tree by devouring its leaves and shoots in a short amount of time. The first sign that your tree has caterpillars is that the leaves appear to be eaten.

It's important to remove them as soon as you see them to prevent any further damage to your tree.

Vine Weevils

Vine weevil larvae feed on your tree's roots, and by the time the symptoms are visible above ground, it's usually too late. Your tree's leaves, twigs, and branches will start wilting as if it hasn't received enough water.

The best way to treat weevils is to prevent them altogether. If you spot an adult weevil, remove them from your tree immediately. You can also rub the outside of the pot with a barrier glue that will prevent them from getting into the pot.

Mealy Bugs

Mealy bugs look like tiny cotton balls on the leaves and branches of your tree. The insects hide inside the little balls, and they're commonly found in clumps. Root mealy bugs can also be found on your tree's root system, so it's important to look out for them when repotting.

If your tree is infested with mealy bugs, your tree will grow very slowly, and the leaves will turn yellow, wilt, droop, and eventually fall off.

How to Treat Pests

The first step is to quarantine the infested tree as quickly as possible to prevent the pests from infesting your other plants or bonsai trees. Most pests can be removed by hand, but you can also use a broad-spectrum pesticide. Depending on the type of pesticide you select, you can add it to the water you give your tree or introduce it into the soil mixture. Be careful to choose the right pesticide for your needs, and seek advice from a reputable vendor, as there is an abundance of different varieties that may be detrimental to the health of your tree. You'll find that there is a wide range of environmentally friendly pesticides on the market.

Common Diseases

Black Spot

Black spot is a fungus that attacks leaves, leaving telltale black spots on the leaf's surface. Once a leaf is infected, it must be removed to stop the infection from spreading. If left, the leaf will turn yellow, shrivel, and fall off.

The best way to treat your tree for black spot is to spray fungicide on the unaffected leaves. Water will spread the spores, so it's important not to water your tree until the fungus is completely gone.

Mold or Mildew

Mildew is a fungus that is found in humid environments without proper ventilation and light. Mildew can be a white powdery substance or a black, spotty mold on your tree's branches and twigs.

Infected leaves and twigs must be removed immediately to prevent the spread of mildew. You can then spray your tree with fungicide.

Leaf Spot

Leaf spot is very similar to black spot. Depending on the species, you'll see white, black, brown, or white spots on the leaves of your tree. The spots usually start out as white and become darker as the infection progresses. Bruising and scarring will then appear before the leaves wither and die.

Rust

Rust is another common fungal disease, and the fungus is red, orange, yellow, or brown. It grows as bumps on the underside of leaves, eventually causing them to curl, die and fall off.

Treat rust by removing the affected leaves and spraying the rest of your tree with fungicide, and remember to place your tree in a well-ventilated area.

Canker Disease

Also known as scab, canker disease can take hold of your tree after pruning. It can also be caused by too much nitrogen in the soil or incorrect fertilizing. Canker disease can be identified by discolored leaves, swollen bark, and slow growth.

To treat it, remove all the affected areas and apply wound sealant. To ensure that your tree doesn't get a canker infection, make sure that you're fertilizing your tree correctly and use clean, sharp tools while pruning.

Chlorosis

Chlorosis is caused by a lack of chlorophyll in your tree's leaves. It's caused by a damaged or compacted root system as well as a deficiency in nutrients, especially iron. Your tree's leaves will turn yellow, but the veins will still be green, and the entire tree will start wilting.

You can add iron chelate to the water used to water your tree to help increase its iron levels. You will also ensure that your tree's root system is well looked after.

Root Rot

Overwatering and insufficient drainage can cause your tree's roots to turn brown and mushy. Above ground, the leaves can lose their color, branches and twigs will become brittle, and your tree's growth will slow down.

You will need to repot your tree using fresh soil after you've pruned away the affected roots. Ensure that the pot has sufficient drainage holes, and always test the soil's moisture before watering.

How to Treat Diseases

As with pests, the first step in treating an infected tree is to place it in quarantine so that it doesn't contaminate your other plants. This is especially true with fungal infections.

Remove the affected areas and spray the unaffected parts of your tree with fungicide. Always check for the possible causes of the infection. Check for root rot, overly damp soil, and ensure that your tree gets enough fresh air.

Once treated, place your tree in a brightly lit, well-ventilated area to prevent reinfection.

Key Takeaways

- It's important to know the signs and symptoms of an unhealthy tree.

- The sooner a tree is treated for pests and infections, the quicker it will recuperate.

- Despite your best efforts, your tree may still pick up a pest or an infection.

- Make sure to quarantine your tree so that the pests or infections aren't spread to your other plants.

- Always use clean and sharp tools when pruning to minimize the risk of infection.

- Make sure that your tree is placed in a well-lit and ventilated spot.

In the next chapter, we'll discuss how to protect your tree from harsh temperatures, extreme weather, and other seasonal changes.

CHAPTER 14

SHELTER AND SEASONAL PREVENTATIVES

Protecting your tree from the elements, especially during the harsh winter months, will ensure that it makes it to spring and is healthy and ready for its growth period. You don't have to have an elaborate, expensive setup. Enough protection from the elements will do just fine.

Not all trees will need the same amount of protection, so it's always important to research your tree's species to find out everything you can about its ideal growing conditions. You also need to take your climate into account. Think about how much sun you get, how hot the summers are, and how cold the winters can be. Do you live in an area that experiences frosty and icy conditions? Do you experience high winds or torrential showers?

All of the factors need to be taken into consideration when setting up a shelter for your tree.

Sun and Heat Protection

 Different species of trees need different amounts of direct sun, but all trees need plenty of light. Without light, a tree's leaves can't photosynthesize. While plenty of trees can survive in full sunlight, others need some shade as well. Exposing shade-loving trees to too much direct sunlight can result in burnt leaves and can be fatal.

It's essential to keep in mind that having your tree exposed to direct sunlight will result in the soil drying out much faster, so you'll need to keep an eye on the moisture levels and water as needed. This may mean that you'll need to water your tree twice a day or more, especially during the summer months.

You can add a layer of moss to the surface of the soil if it's drying out too quickly. Moss will help the soil retain water and will prevent surface roots from drying out. If moss isn't available, you can also use other organic materials like straw, bark, or shredded untreated paper or cardboard.

If you notice that your tree is struggling in the sun, move it to a place where it can get direct sunlight in the morning and late afternoons but where it can get shade during the hottest part of the day.

If it's possible, you can also build an inexpensive covering for your tree using shade cloth. Shade cloth is available at most garden centers and hardware stores, and you can choose the percentage of sun that it blocks. Shade cloth is particularly helpful when your tree needs light but not direct sunlight. A fine mesh netting will also work well to block out the sun's rays.

Wind Protection

 Wind can break branches and twigs, dry out the soil very quickly or, worst of all, make the pot fall over and potentially damage your tree. Bonsai trees are particularly susceptible to the wind because they are not anchored firmly into the ground.

If you're placing your tree outside, think about where the wind usually comes from and how strong it is. Do you live in an area where you experience strong winds? Or do you live in an area that has hot, dry winds that can quickly dry out the soil?

The first step to protecting your tree from the wind is to ensure that the tree is secured in its pot. You can also place your tree in a spot where it is sheltered from the wind. Many practitioners will place their trees on the ground up against a solid structure like the wall of a house or garage. Alternatively, you can build a partial barrier to protect your tree using inexpensive materials that are readily available. Another tip is to weigh the pot itself down by using rocks or stones to add more weight to the base of the tree.

Rain Protection

 While rainwater is perfectly healthy for your tree, it's the quantity of water that may cause a problem, especially if your area is prone to heavy rainfall. Too much rain can make the soil become water-logged and can result in root rot, so it's essential to make sure that the pot has sufficient drainage holes.

If your tree is placed outside and you're experiencing heavy rains, check on it regularly to make sure that the soil isn't waterlogged. You might need to consider placing your tree under a shelter if extended periods of rainfall are predicted. You can also tip the pot slightly to remove any excess water that has collected in the soil.

Protecting Your Tree in Winter

 When winter is approaching, you may want to take extra precautions to protect your tree from the elements. This is especially true if your tree isn't native to your area and it's placed outside.

If your tree is native to your area, it should have less of a problem spending the winter months outside as it's built for the normal seasonal cycle. The only exception is if exceptionally harsh winter conditions are predicted. Because your bonsai tree is planted in a shallow pot, the roots will be more susceptible to frostbite, which can kill your tree.

Most trees will go dormant in winter. Deciduous trees will lose their leaves, and evergreen trees will slow down their growth. Many bonsai enthusiasts place their trees in an unheated garage or shed during the winter. The idea behind this is to keep the tree from experiencing the daily freezing and thawing of the ground to protect the shallow roots.

Because the tree is dormant, it won't need as much sunlight as it does in its growing months. Too much sun exposure will unnecessarily dry out the soil. Although it's still necessary to water your tree in the winter, you don't need to give it fertilizer because of its dormancy.

Non-native trees will need extra protection. Tropical and subtropical trees, like the Ficus, will need to be brought indoors for the winter. Place them in a warm but well-ventilated spot that gets plenty of light. In the Northern hemisphere, this will most likely be near a south-facing window and a north-facing window in the Southern hemisphere.

Key Takeaways

- If your tree is native to your area, it will be able to withstand normal local weather conditions.

- Trees need protection from extreme sun, heat, wind, and rain.

- In winter, make sure to protect your tree's root system from frostbite.

- Trees are dormant in the winter months, so they don't need fertilizer, but they'll still need water.

- Tropical and subtropical trees will need to be indoors in the winter.

In the next chapter, we'll be comparing young trees and mature trees and helping you to decide which option is best for you!

CHAPTER 15

YOUNG TREES VS. MATURE TREES

Young Trees

A young tree is a great, inexpensive way for a beginner bonsai enthusiast to learn the ropes. Because they're so young, they're a lot more forgiving, allowing beginners to make a few mistakes along the way without serious consequences. Saplings are relatively cheap, and you'll be able to source them from most nurseries and garden centers.

Buying Nursery Stock

Buying a pre-bonsai tree or sapling is much more cost-effective than buying an already-established bonsai tree. Caring for a pre-bonsai tree will also teach you much more about the art of bonsai and tree maintenance in general.

Young trees and saplings are commonly referred to as nursery stock within bonsai circles. It's usually best to look for nursery stock at small, independently owned nurseries or garden centers. Most nurseries will have the best stock in the early spring and through the summer.

When buying nursery stock, you'll need to have a species in mind, along with the shape or style that you'd most like to achieve. This will help you narrow down the sometimes-overwhelming number of choices you'll be faced with. Buying a tree with naturally interesting features will accelerate the development process. Regardless of your desired outcome, the most important thing is to select a healthy tree.

Mature Trees

Purchasing a mature tree is the preferred way to start the bonsai journey for most beginners. Let's take a look at what you should consider when purchasing a mature tree.

Where to Buy a Mature Bonsai Tree

Large nurseries and garden centers tend to have a bonsai section where you can find a good selection of bonsai trees. They might not always be in great shape because of the specialized care that they need, so you'll need to look out for signs of under- or over-watering and pests and disease, which we already discussed in a previous chapter.

Most bonsai beginners will either purchase an already-established tree or receive one as a gift. A mature tree is a great way to learn the basics of bonsai care, maintenance, and styling. Once you learn these basics, you'll be more confident to cultivate and create a bonsai from scratch.

You can also find specialized online bonsai stores which deliver throughout a certain area. These trees tend to be in much better condition, and a great deal of care is taken to ensure that they arrive on your doorstep in great shape. They do tend to be more expensive than the trees available at a nursery.

Things to Look for When Buying a Bonsai Tree

When looking to buy a bonsai tree, think about where you'd like to place it and what your climate is like. For example, you may want to purchase a Ficus and want to place it outside, but you live in a cold area. Ficus trees are subtropical, so they need lots of warmth and sunlight, so indoors is usually the best place for them.

Keep in mind the space that you have available, whether it's indoors or outdoors. Some bonsai trees can be up to six feet tall! If you have a small apartment, you won't necessarily have the space for the size pot that such a tall tree needs. The bigger the tree, the heavier it'll be, so if you need to repot your tree or move it around, you'll need to keep your own physical limitations in mind too.

When buying a mature tree, you'll be able to prune and wire some existing branches, but the root ball and the trunk are already established, so it will be more challenging to make changes in that area. Look for a tree with a trunk that appeals to you.

If you're a beginner, look for a tree that's easy to care for. If you're starting out and you buy a high-maintenance tree, you may become disheartened if the tree dies, so start out easy. As you gain more knowledge and your bonsai skills improve, you'll be able to move on to more high-maintenance trees. The most popular trees for beginners are

- Ficus
- Chinese elm
- small leaf jade
- juniper

Don't be in a rush to buy. Research the species that you're interested in to make sure that you're able to meet all the requirements it needs.

It's always important to check the tree for signs of disease or pests. Make sure it's showing signs of growth, like buds and leaves, and that the pot is in good shape. The signs of a healthy bonsai tree are

- bright green leaves without any discoloration.
- a smooth, tapered trunk.
- roots are slightly showing.
- proportionate and symmetrical branches.
- no crossed roots or branches.

Key Takeaways

- Independent nurseries and garden centers are the best places to get good pre-bonsai trees.

- Nursery stock is usually available from early spring to late summer. You can buy mature bonsai trees from nurseries, garden centers, or specialized online bonsai stores. Please bear in mind unless you are given a mature tree as a gift, acquiring a mature bonsai is the most expensive and high-risk approach to take when starting out.

- Consider where you'd like to place your tree, how much space you have available, and the size of the tree you like.

- Start your bonsai journey with an easy-to-care-for tree.

- Before buying your tree, make sure it's healthy and free of pests or diseases.

Growing your bonsai tree from seed is a commitment with a great reward. Not only is it cost-effective, but it allows you to be involved in your tree's development from day one. Let's take a look at all you need to know to grow your bonsai tree from seed.

CHAPTER 16

GROWING FROM SEED

M*isho* is the Japanese term for growing a bonsai tree from a seed, and it's a great way to slowly start your journey into the art of bonsai. As your seed sprouts, becomes a sapling and starts growing, so will your knowledge and expertise!

Growing your bonsai tree from seed will take time and patience. It can be up to four years before you can start styling your tree, but the rewards will be undeniable.

Advantages and Disadvantages of Growing From Seed

Growing your bonsai tree from seeds is usually the most cost-effective method. Seeds are less expensive than saplings or mature trees. You can also take your time in purchasing the specialized tools you'll need because you won't need to prune it until it's old enough.

When you start pruning and shaping your tree, it will be much easier to do due to its young age. With a mature tree or even a sapling, your pruning may have to be more radical because you'll need to re-train what's already been established.

Growing your bonsai tree from seeds gives you full control over your tree's environment from day one. You'll be able to track its development, and the sense of satisfaction you'll have can't be compared to anything else.

As you can imagine, growing your bonsai tree will require time and patience. Trees don't grow overnight, so you may need to remind yourself of the end goal as you're waiting for your seedling to be mature enough to start shaping and styling.

Sprouts and seedlings are extremely delicate, so you'll need to be extra careful with them. You'll have to protect them from the elements and ensure that your fertilizer isn't too strong.

Many bonsai beginners like to buy a mature tree, but plant seeds at the same time, giving themselves the best of both worlds. You can practice styling and shaping your mature tree while waiting for your seeds to germinate and the seedlings to develop.

Where to Get Seeds

Many people are under the incorrect assumption that you can buy bonsai seeds. As you know, a bonsai tree is genetically identical to its full-grown counterparts, so it will grow from exactly the same seeds as a full-grown tree.

You can get seeds from your local nursery or garden center, as well as specialized online bonsai stores. If you're interested in growing a tree that's native to your area, you can also collect seeds from your surroundings. Native trees are suited to their climate, so they tend to be easier to maintain.

When to Plant

If you've collected seeds from your surroundings, you can plant them in the autumn. If you've ordered seeds for non-native trees, you'll need to use stratification techniques to prepare them for planting.

What Is Stratification?

Stratification is the process of imitating a seed's ideal conditions for germination. The seeds of many species of trees go through a cold period during the winter before they germinate. If you live in a warm area or if you want to plant out of season, you'll need to put the seeds through that cold period yourself. For most seeds, this means you'll need to soak them in water for 24 hours before placing them in the fridge for a month or two. The exact amount of time and the temperature all depend on the species, so you'll need to look it up before continuing.

How to Plant

Planting seeds is as easy as putting in a pot with soil, but there are a few tips and tricks that you can keep in mind to make things even easier.

You can use a pot or a seedling tray to plant your seed; the choice is up to you. A pot will give your seedling a lot more room to grow before it needs to be repotted, whereas you'll need to repot your seedling relatively soon if it's confined to a seedling tray. Either way, be sure that the container you choose has sufficient drainage.

Place a layer of gravel at the bottom of your container to encourage draining, and fill the remainder with nutrient-rich potting or bonsai soil mixture. Once it germinates, the seed will need plenty of nutrients to help it grow. Make sure that the soil isn't compressed too tightly. The seed needs space to expand when it germinates.

Using your finger, poke a few holes in the soil. Make sure the holes are well-spaced so that your seeds don't overcrowd each other when they start germinating. Pop the seeds in the holes and cover them with a thin layer of soil. The rule of thumb is that seeds need half their length in soil covering them. If they're planted too deep, they won't germinate at all.

Water the soil until it's damp. It's best to use a spray bottle or a fine nozzle, so the soil covering the seeds isn't disturbed. Place the container in a well-ventilated area that gets good light but not necessarily direct sunlight. Monitor the soil's moisture level to ensure it doesn't dry out.

If your tree is native to your area and you planted the seeds in the autumn, you can expect germination and sprouting in the early spring. If you're keeping your seed container indoors, you may see germination and sprouting as early as four weeks.

You can start fertilizing your seedlings about six weeks after they sprout but be sure to use a very diluted solution. The seedlings can easily get burnt with fertilizer that's too strong.

After the first year, you can separate the seedlings and place each of them in their own pots. Allow the seedlings to grow for at least a year before starting to prune and style them.

Key Takeaways

- Growing a bonsai tree from seeds takes time and patience.

- You can buy seeds online or at your local nursery or garden center.

- You can also collect seeds from your surroundings if you're interested in growing a tree native to your area.

- Non-native seeds may need to go through the stratification process.

Nurturing a seed is a satisfying and inexpensive way to add to your bonsai collection. But what could be better than acquiring more mature bonsai trees, absolutely free and within a fraction of the time?

In the following chapters, we'll show you how to do just that!

CHAPTER 17

FREE TREES
PART 1—YAMADORI

We all like to discover things that are free in life, and free bonsai trees are no exception. In the next two chapters, we will discuss two easy ways that you, too, can source free bonsai material from in and around your local area.

Not only will these two new methods provide endless possibilities for expanding your bonsai collection, but they will also provide you with an opportunity to work with trees you may not have considered to be traditional bonsai material.

Due to rising global import costs, there has been a growing trend by many to look to utilize the trees they find naturally around them. This, in turn, has created unique and fantastic bonsai trees.

The first technique we will consider is the traditional technique of *yamadori*.

Yamadori

If you haven't heard of the term before, *yamadori* simply means the process of sourcing and collecting wild-grown trees. "Dori" roughly translates to "dug or taken," and "Yama" means "mountain," so "taken from the mountain."

Traditionally wild trees would be sourced and collected from remote areas high in the mountains and around rugged coastal areas. Due to these harsh environments, the trees are exposed to fierce winds and harsh conditions for decades. In turn, those elemental factors shape and create beautiful and unique trees without any human interference.

These mature trees would then be sought after, collected, and carried back home over long distances. The trees gathered would then be provided with the right conditions to thrive in order to refine them into amazing bonsai.

Sadly, we don't all live in remote mountainous areas to find amazing trees, but that doesn't mean we can't find great trees locally. In recent years a trend that's sprung up, known as *Urban Yamadori* has seen a huge rise in popularity.

If you haven't already guessed, then this is where trees are sourced and found locally, in and around woodland areas, parks, private land, hedgerows, and gardens.

Throughout this book, we have mentioned that bonsai is an art form, and there aren't always hard and fast rules that you have to stick to. However, there is one rule we must ask that you adhere to at all times, and that is to always seek permission from the landowner. We want everyone to enjoy bonsai, and we don't want anyone to find themselves in trouble by taking trees that they haven't had permission to collect. Please, always seek permission before proceeding. Areas of natural beauty will be protected under local laws, so please be careful when searching out new trees.

With that disclaimer out of the way, we will now look at how you, too, can identify and collect trees safely to make your own amazing bonsai for free.

In order to maximize the potential of any tree collected and ensure the health of the tree, there are a few simple steps and tools required.

Locating a Suitable Tree

There can be some real gems in your own existing garden that you may never have considered as bonsai. You may know someone who is looking to remove a section of hedgerow, or you know someone with wild areas of land in which to explore, and the owner is happy for you to collect several trees at once.

Regardless of location, you are looking for trees that have interesting features and that are pleasing to the eye. Wild trees are rarely refined, but it is good to picture what the potential final results will be when initially selecting a tree. The overall thing to remember is shape and style can be worked into the tree over time, but the main point at this stage is to find a healthy tree free from pests and disease.

In a previous chapter, we discussed the optimal time to repot, and *yamadori* trees are no different. Wild trees are mainly collected around this same time period when the trees are coming out of their winter dormancy and showing signs of new buds starting to swell.

Once you have found a suitable tree, you will need to plan ahead.

The next step to success is to gather the right tools you will need to extract the tree you have identified. Digging up trees can be a very physically demanding task and not one that should be taken lightly. Trees that have substantial root mass require a lot of effort to remove. With this in mind, you may wish to invite a friend to help you collect and share the workload.

It's always important to keep hydrated and to know your limits. The tree isn't going anywhere, so you have plenty of time to prepare and uproot.

Practical tools that you will need for success are a digging spade with a sharp edge. A pair of shears to help prune back and free any vegetation around the tree. These can also double up to help cut and free stubborn finer roots. For larger roots, a saw would be preferable to help cut through the thicker root mass.

You will also need several garbage bags to wrap and protect the root system. A simple piece of wire or tape can secure the bag around the root base, making it easier to extract without causing damage while protecting the tree on the journey home. In order to carry all these tools at once, it's advisable to find a suitable carry bag. Not only will this make traveling much easier, but once the tree is collected, you will be able to use the bag to attach and carry the tree safely while being hands-free.

Suitable clothing, a hat, sunglasses, and safe, strong boots for digging are highly recommended. Some trees come out relatively easily, but others can take several hours, so please remember to take enough food and water. To stay safe, always carry first aid supplies, and if exploring areas off the beaten track, ensure somebody knows where you are planning on traveling prior to setting out.

The next step is the fun part, extraction!

Extracting Yamadori

You've found your tree, it's the right time of year, and you have all the gear needed, so now what? The first thing is to ensure a clear workspace. A tree may be solitary and easily accessible, but some can be very tricky to get in and around the base due to vegetation or other hazards getting in the way. Potentially this is not something that will be a problem in your garden, but out in remote locations, this can hamper progress and make the task a lot harder if not prepared. It's not always easy, but try to clear a large area above and around the tree and be mindful of hazards that may impede digging.

Once cleared, try to visualize the root mass that you will need to extract. A good way to figure this out is to look at the overall width of the tree's canopy and longest branches. The root system underneath will roughly be the same diameter as what is shown above ground.

Start by digging around the outskirts of the tree in a circular fashion. Each time digging a little closer and deeper toward the tree's base. You will find the soil and roots start to become looser, and it then becomes easier to identify the main root mass. With some trees, just digging in this fashion is enough to free the tree and the root ball fairly quickly. It's rarely that straightforward, and many trees have strong root systems that are hard to free and require more persuasion. Many trees have strong structural roots that work out radially from the tree and need to be cut or sawn through depending on thickness. When cutting these larger roots, try to take care not to harm as many of the fibrous roots as possible.

Once the tree is free from the ground, give yourself a quick pat on the back and move on to the final step.

When you dig up a tree in this manner, the goal is to reserve the root mass with minimal disturbance. Try to leave as much of the original soil intact as possible; sometimes, this is referred to as "mountain soil" in recognition of traditional *yamadori*.

The main goal now is to work quickly in order to secure the tree safely and stop any of the roots that are now exposed to air from drying out. This is where your cheap garbage bags come in handy. If you are collecting a tree from your garden, let's say, it's advisable to water the roots to moisten them before wrapping the whole root mass of the tree within plastic bags. This helps retain moisture and protects the roots. This can be challenging, though, when collecting out in the field. Carrying extra water with you for this purpose is recommended but can add substantial weight to an already heavy load. Being prepared beforehand and not taking too long before returning home with your collected tree is key in circumstances where you find you have little to no access to water.

Once home, it's then a case of watering the whole root mass and allowing the tree to recover. You can now treat this collected tree in the same manner as you would treat any other bonsai tree. Please refer to the chapters earlier in the book about bringing your tree home and repotting.

If you think *yamadori* is an amazing way to source trees, you are going to love the next chapter!

CHAPTER 18

FREE TREES PART 2 —AIR LAYERING

The technique of air layering has been around for hundreds of years and has changed very little since its inception. It's always struck us as a magical process, and one that can enhance anyone's skill set and bonsai collection once mastered.

The simplicity of air layering is truly the best part, and it allows the practitioner to duplicate and recreate a new tree from existing material that you may already have.

The time in which a new, high-quality bonsai tree can be created shouldn't be underestimated, and it is widely practiced in bonsai circles.

Below, we will teach you how to successfully create your own trees using the method of air layering so you, too, can learn this fantastic bonsai secret.

What Is Air Layering?

To get the best results and the most success from this technique, you will need to understand what the overall goal is first and how air layering works.

Air layering or propagation isn't just used solely on bonsai trees. This method can be used on plants, shrubs, fruit-bearing trees, and many other species.

The idea of this method is to shock the parent tree by making a series of cuts to a selected branch or section of the trunk, removing the outer layers of bark all the way down, just past the cambium layer. You may recall during our Trees 101 Chapter at the beginning of the book, we discussed the different layers that make up a tree's trunk and branches. The cambium layer's function is to grow new bark and wood as it receives hormones known as *auxins*.

Removing this soft cambium layer forces the section above the cut site to fight for survival, and over a short period of time, this section will then start to produce its own fibrous roots mid-way up the tree.

Once the roots have developed and matured, the branch or section can then be separated from the parent tree and repotted.

Thus, creating a new tree for free and, in some cases, a very worthy and established-looking bonsai tree.

You will still be left with the original tree, and if the opportunity presents itself, the process can be carried out repeatedly with little to no disturbance to the parent tree. We advise you to let the parent tree recover and grow once more before attempting the process again. You could expand your collection rapidly using this method.

Many specialist bonsai suppliers use this technique to replenish their stock levels saving on import costs and time.

A good example of a tree that is great for this technique is the Japanese maple. Most young trees grow tall and are very slender, especially when starting out, and the maple is no exception. Having a thicker trunk at the base that tapers and reduces as you make your way up the tree is always a desirable attribute when creating a bonsai. Maples air layer extremely easily and quickly, and they are one of the better-known and successful types of bonsai trees on which to try this technique.

By allowing a young tree to grow tall, it encourages the base and trunk to grow thicker and stronger to support the weight of the canopy. Eventually, once the tree's trunk reaches the desired thickness, you will then typically proceed to cut it back to a much lower starting point, sometimes referred to as a *trunk chop*. This will naturally produce taper over time, and a new leader will then start to grow at the cut site. A leader is the thinner new growth that will eventually over time, become thicker and form the main branch or trunk of the tree once again. This gives the tree a mature look over time, and this can be repeated over many years.

However, instead of just cutting back to a section, many enthusiasts use the technique of air layering not only to produce a thickening effect but to gain additional bonsai material for future development. You will still achieve the effect you desire on the parent tree but gain a free tree in doing so.

If you imagine a thick branch on a tree separating and becoming that new tree's trunk, you will be able to understand the endless possibilities you have at your fingertips.

Air layering can go wrong, however, if not done correctly, and you could lose the section you are trying to separate. You may even damage the parent tree in the process, leaving it with a nasty scar, making it vulnerable to disease, or even killing it outright.

Let's now look at the seven techniques required to safely create your own piece of air-layering magic.

Air-Layering Technique

Identifying a suitable cut zone on your given tree.

When thinking about making a future tree from existing stock, it's preferable to look at a section or branch that is interesting to the eye. We know that shaping and styling are desirable, so we want to try and avoid straight sections and areas with undesirable features. This maximizes the potential of the new bonsai and gives it a more mature, interesting look from the start.

Preparing to make the cut.

Once you've located a suitable branch, you will need to make a series of cuts to initiate the process. This can be a dangerous and difficult task because it requires the use of a sharp cutting tool or knife, and the surrounding branches can impede and limit access. Ensure the tool used is sharp enough to make smooth, clean cuts, reducing the risk of the blade slipping. We would advise you to wear a thick pair of gardening gloves or similar at this stage and ensure the area is clear of hazards before proceeding.

Making the cut.

The next step is to make two separate circular cuts around the selected branch, and you will need to space these cuts apart. A good guide to know how far is to ensure that the distance is at least the thickness of the branch itself. So, for example, if the branch is one inch thick, the distance between the top cut and bottom cut should be around two inches, giving you plenty of leeway. The distance between cuts is key to ensuring the best success. The cut made furthest away from the main body of the tree will be the area in which the new roots form. Leaving a large enough gap will ensure the tree can't heal or reform after the cut process is completed.

Once these two initial circular cuts have been made, another single cut is made, bridging the gap between and connecting the two original cuts. This, in turn, will then allow you to start to peel away the section of bark in one complete piece and motion, removing everything down to and including the cambium layer.

You will then be left with a very pale-looking section that is clearly defined on the branch. It's important to ensure this section is completely free of the outer layers of bark at this stage before moving on

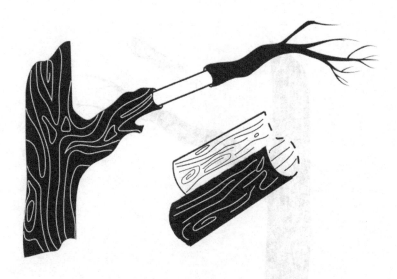

Preparing the new area for success.

Now that the difficult part is out of the way, you will need to prepare the new area to produce the best results and increase the chance the air layer will root. In order for the new roots to form, there needs to be a medium in which they can grow and thrive. Sphagnum moss has been used for centuries and is a fantastic natural resource that can aid with tree health and recovery, and it can also speed up the air layering process.

Sphagnum moss can be found in naturally damp or boggy areas but can also be bought from most reputable garden suppliers.

The moisture retention properties it holds are key to ensuring the new roots receive enough water throughout while also having something to bind with.

At this stage, you may wish to treat the section with a hormone-rooting powder or gel to aid with development first before moving on. However, this is optional, and not every bonsai enthusiast agrees this is necessary for the air layer to be successful.

The tree will naturally look to survive and produce the new roots needed, but applying treatment beforehand is seen as an insurance policy and one that many swear by.

Regardless of the option you decide to choose, the new section will now need to be wrapped and protected in a ball of sphagnum moss.

Securing the air layer in position.

Sphagnum moss won't stick or bind around the tree for very long, and it will quickly fall away, so we need to ensure that we contain and wrap the contents so that there is little to no disturbance to the fine roots that will form.

There are several methods by which we can achieve this that are inexpensive and proven to work.

The first and easiest method is to wrap a ball of damp moss around the cut site and then, in turn, wrap the ball using a clear plastic liner or bag. The bag is then tied to the tree with a piece of wire to secure it in place. The plastic will protect the moss inside and increase the humidity levels, which is desirable and beneficial for the roots to form. Always ensure the moss is making contact with the exposed area before wrapping.

Another easy method is to take a plastic plant pot and cut it in half. The two pieces can then be placed on either side of the cut site and secured with wire in position once again. The pot can be easily filled with sphagnum moss and wrapped in the same manner as before.

There is also a new method on the market that utilizes air layering pods. These have been designed specifically to aid in this process. Similar to the plastic plant pot method, the pods unclip and reunite around the cut section, allowing them to be filled with moss. They are great because they can be bought in different sizes to suit the needs of the branch in question, and they can be used repeatedly over many seasons. You will find these easily online and from many reputable garden centers.

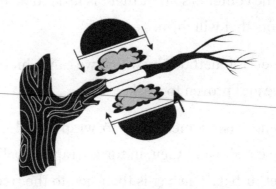

Checking in and maintaining your newly formed air layer.
The advantage of using clear plastic is that it allows you to check in on the progress of the new roots forming, and you can also tell when the moss may be drying out and needs topping up with fresh water.

The length of time you leave the moss around the cut site varies from tree to tree and your own local growing conditions. You may see new roots forming quickly after a couple of weeks, but it's best to wait until you see a larger mass of strong-looking roots before attempting to remove the air layer. Typically, this will take around 6–10 weeks on average for most species to fully form the root mass needed to support the new section. Please bear in mind that species like pines can be notorious for not taking root at all, and even then, the air layer may need to be left on for a year or more before it can be safely removed.

The optimal time for most species to attempt the air layering technique is when the leaves have hardened off and fully developed, and it's moving from late spring into the early summer months.

Removing and repotting your newly formed tree.

One of the best feelings you can experience in bonsai is when you know that you have successfully created new life and a new tree.

Be careful not to disturb the root mass, prune, or saw below the root ball, and carefully remove the new section from the parent tree. Make sure you seal any cuts on the original tree to protect the new area from infection.

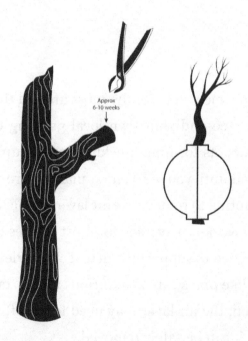

Your newly formed bonsai will need a little more care than most due to the delicate new roots. You can go ahead and gently re-move the outer plastic wrapping while trying not to disturb the sphagnum moss as much as possible. The tree can then be planted with the moss directly in a training pot or container with a good substrate. The tree will then need to be placed in a shady spot and watered regularly until you see the vigor of the tree spring to life. It won't be long before you start to see newly formed buds or leaves. You now have a brand-new bonsai tree that you can enjoy developing for years to come, and it hasn't cost you a penny.

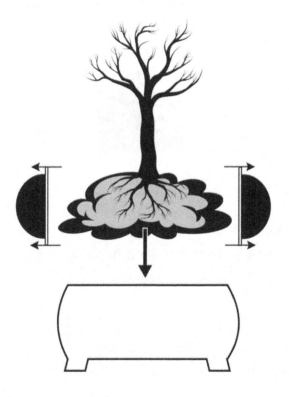

The possibilities to create new and existing trees for free are never-ending.

CHAPTER 19

JOINING A CLUB OR ASSOCIATION

Sharing knowledge and information is the best way to learn. By joining a bonsai club, be it in person or online, you can expand your skills and make new friends!

Benefits of Joining a Bonsai Club

Learning From Experienced Members

Learning from those who have more experience is possibly one of the greatest benefits of joining a bonsai club. Club members will usually have a wide range of skills, from beginners to lifelong practitioners. Experienced members will be able to provide guidance, tips, and advice on all aspects of bonsai, such as choosing a tree, pruning, wiring, and preparing a tree for harsh weather. One huge advantage of joining a local club is that the members you meet will all be facing the same challenges in regard to climate and pest problems, and you will automatically gain access to their wisdom on these topics to help you with your own trees.

Access to Resources

When you're starting out in bonsai, you might not have all the tools and materials you'll need. Many clubs have a shared collection of tools and equipment that members can borrow for a time. Clubs may also have a library of books, magazines, and videos that can provide valuable information.

Opportunities to Participate in Events

Bonsai clubs will usually organize workshops or other events where members can learn new skills, exchange ideas, or showcase their trees. Workshops can focus on one of the many aspects of bonsai, from pruning and wiring to styling and soil mixtures. Events can include bonsai exhibitions or trips to tree auctions. Participating in these events is a great way to get inspiration for your own bonsai journey.

Socializing With Like-Minded People

Bonsai enthusiasts come from all walks of life, and bonsai clubs tend to be meeting places for a diverse range of people. You'll be able to connect with people who share your passion at social events like dinners, holiday parties, and picnics hosted by the club.

Accountability and Motivation

Bonsai is a solitary pastime, and it's easy to become discouraged and lose motivation. Joining a bonsai club can help you to stay committed and motivated, even if you face challenges. Sharing your challenges with the community can help you find clarity and inspiration.

How to Find a Bonsai Club

To find a bonsai club near you, there are a number of things that you can do. First, you can do a quick Google search to look for bonsai clubs in your area. Check social media platforms like Facebook and Instagram for bonsai clubs. Most clubs will have a social media presence. Alternatively, you can join bonsai-related groups or pages and ask for recommendations. These online communities are a great resource and provide a wealth of information even if you are unable to access a physical bonsai club or association.

Visit nurseries in your area that specialize in bonsai. They may have information about local clubs as well as bulletin boards or newsletters with details of upcoming bonsai events. Bonsai exhibitions and workshops are usually organized by local clubs, and attending these events can be a great way to connect with other enthusiasts and learn about which clubs are in the area.

National or regional bonsai associations often keep lists of affiliated clubs, which can be a useful resource for finding a local club. You can contact these associations by phone or email and ask for information about clubs in your area.

Once you've identified one or more bonsai clubs in your area, reach out to them and ask about membership, events, and activities. Most clubs welcome new members and are happy to provide information and support to beginners. But please don't despair if you find there are no clubs in your area. With this book and access to the previously mentioned online forums and groups, you still have everything you need at your fingertips to get started and succeed in bonsai!

Key Takeaways

- Joining a bonsai club will allow you to meet people who share the same interests as you.

- Many clubs offer courses and workshops.

- Online bonsai clubs will allow you to meet people from all over the world and are great if you don't have a physical club in your local area.

For us, finding a club, be it physical or online, is easily one of the most rewarding and useful steps you can take as a budding bonsai practitioner. It will speed up your progress, advance your learning, and you may even make some great new friends along the way.

CONCLUSION

So, you've come a long way since page one. You have learned a wealth of information, and your bonsai journey is well underway. Throughout this book, we have aimed to equip you with the confidence and skills necessary to branch out on your own into the world of bonsai.

As you will know by now, bonsai is a rewarding hobby that offers you opportunities to explore your creativity, learn something new, and even practice mindfulness. Whether you're just starting out or a long-time enthusiast, there's always something new to learn and experience.

In this book, we've covered the fundamentals of bonsai that will serve as your knowledge base as a beginner or as a refresher if you've been collecting and training bonsai for some time.

You've discovered the different classifications of trees and learned a little more about the species that are most suitable for bonsai. You've also seen a number of different and interesting styles that you can shape your tree into, from beginner-friendly to more complex.

You've also gone through all the components that will help you to successfully grow and care for your own bonsai tree—from the soil, water, and fertilizer to the pot itself. You now have a better understanding of both pruning and wiring and which tools you'll need to maintain your tree.

You've also acquired knowledge on how to maintain the health of your tree. We've discussed the variety of pests and diseases that your tree is susceptible to, as well as ways in which to treat them.

You've also seen that your tree may need protection from the elements as the seasons change or when extreme weather is predicted—not to mention the chapters covering air layering, *yamadori*, and growing new trees from seeds. These chapters alone will ensure that you never need to worry about sourcing expensive trees.

Your bonsai tree is a living work of art, and you're responsible for its health and longevity. It's your responsibility to care for it and treat it with respect. In doing so, you can achieve a sense of peace and accomplishment as you apply your skills and watch your tree flourish. Many long-time enthusiasts will wholeheartedly agree that practicing the art of bonsai has lessened their stress and anxiety.

Bonsai isn't always easy, and it will require patience and perseverance, as well as a certain level of skill and knowledge. It's important to view these challenges as temporary and as an opportunity to learn something new, not just about your tree or bonsai, but about yourself.

Ultimately, bonsai can provide you with numerous opportunities to learn, grow, and connect with nature. With patience, dedication, and a willingness to learn, anyone can become a successful bonsai enthusiast.

As this book comes to an end, you're encouraged to continue on your bonsai journey with a sense of curiosity. Regardless of your skill level, there is always something new to discover and appreciate.

Thank you for taking the time to read *Bonsai For All*. We hope that this book will serve you well for many years to come. Please don't forget to take advantage of the seasonal bonsai calendar we have at the back of this book. This handy guide will act as a helpful companion on your continued journey and help to ensure you do the right things at the right time.

All the very best from everyone at RJJ Publishing!

SEASONAL BONSAI CALENDAR

This Calendar is intended to be a handy quick reference guide to help you make informed decisions throughout the year regarding the care of your bonsai trees.

However, it is crucial that you take the time to <u>research your tree's specific needs</u> and <u>consider the unique nature of your local environment and settings.</u>

The calendar is divided in half, one half will guide people in the northern hemisphere of the globe and the other will help the people in the southern hemisphere.

The calendar outlines nine key action points you will need to consider each month including repotting, pruning, and watering to name a few.

You can easily refer back to the relevant chapters in this book to learn more about all those important bonsai topics, as and when you need to.

Northern Hemisphere

January

- **Repotting** – generally considered too early due to colder weather.
- **Watering** – due to the slow growth rate at this time of year watering will be required less frequently.
- **Feeding** - the vast majority of trees are still dormant, feeding is generally not required during the winter months.
- **Pruning** – ideal time to review your trees and plan for future pruning.
- **Wiring** –check for it biting in, reapply if necessary, and remove if no longer required
- **Root Work** – avoid unless emergency repotting.
- **Pests & Diseases** – periodically check your trees for any signs of ill health and pests.
- **Shelter** – continue to shelter your trees from potential freezing temperatures.
- **Maintenance** – sharpen tools, stock up on supplies for the season ahead.

<u>**Southern Hemisphere**</u>

January

- <u>**Repotting**</u> – emergency repotting only
- <u>**Watering**</u> – monitor moisture levels carefully, increase watering to more than once per day if needed.
- <u>**Feeding**</u> - increase feeding volume and frequency on all trees now they are well into their growing season.
- <u>**Pruning**</u> – time to prune back any unwanted growth and maintain the shape with regular trimming.
- <u>**Wiring**</u> – Be careful when wiring as foliage can be damaged. Check existing wire, adjust and remove if required.
- <u>**Root Work**</u> – no root work required unless there is a specific root related health concern.
- <u>**Pests & Diseases**</u> – as temperatures increase, be extra vigilant to check for bugs and pests, apply insecticide as needed. Remove any damaged or infected foliage or branches to avoid the risk of spreading.
- <u>**Shelter**</u> – heat and wind protection may now be a concern, ensure trees are shaded and secure as needed.
- <u>**Maintenance**</u> – great time to take cuttings for future propagation, ensure tools are sharp and clean, continue diligent moss removal and weeding.

Northern Hemisphere

February

- **Repotting** – considered the best time to repot ahead of new buds forming in spring.
- **Watering** – continue to monitor and increase watering if required.
- **Feeding** – trees will soon start to awaken from dormancy, but it is considered too early to start a feeding regime at this early stage.
- **Pruning** – ideal time to review your trees and plan for future pruning.
- **Wiring** –check for it biting in, reapply if necessary, and remove if no longer required
- **Root Work** – root pruning will be required if considering repotting a specific tree this year. Please refer to the repotting chapter of this book
- **Pests & Diseases** – periodically check your trees for any new signs of ill health and pests.
- **Shelter** – continue to protect your tree from the elements and any cold snaps.
- **Maintenance** – prepare, clean and ready any pots to be used in advance.

<u>**Southern Hemisphere**</u>

February

- **<u>Repotting</u>** – emergency repotting only
- **<u>Watering</u>** – monitor moisture levels carefully, increase watering to more than once per day if needed.
- **<u>Feeding</u>** - maintain feeding volume and frequency as trees approach end of summer.
- **<u>Pruning</u>** – time to prune back any unwanted growth and maintain the shape with regular trimming.
- **<u>Wiring</u>** – Be careful when wiring as foliage can be damaged. Check existing wire, adjust and remove if required.
- **<u>Root Work</u>** – no root work required unless there is a specific root related health concern.
- **<u>Pests & Diseases</u>** – as temperatures increase, be extra vigilant to check for bugs and pests, apply insecticide as needed. Remove any damaged or infected foliage or branches to avoid the risk of spreading.
- **<u>Shelter</u>** – heat and wind protection may now be a concern, ensure trees are shaded and secure as needed.
- **<u>Maintenance</u>** – great time to take cuttings for future propagation, ensure tools are sharp and clean, continue diligent moss removal and weeding.

March

- **Repotting** – now is the key time to repot if you haven't already started.
- **Watering** – frequency begins to increase due to the onset of the growing season.
- **Feeding** – small doses of fertilizer can be introduced to trees that have not been re-potted. Don't feed recently re-potted trees util they have had adequate time to recover. Approximately wait at least 3-4 weeks before applying any feed.
- **Pruning** – only carry out light pruning if necessary to avoid damaging new growth.
- **Wiring** –check for it biting in, reapply if necessary, and remove if no longer required
- **Root Work** – avoid removing large sections of root mass if structural pruning is required at this time..
- **Pests & Diseases** – periodically check your trees for any signs of ill health and pests.
- **Shelter** – continue to shelter your trees, beware of late frosts.
- **Maintenance** – check for and remove weeds and moss. Stock up on fertilizer.

March

- **<u>Repotting</u>** – emergency repotting only
- **<u>Watering</u>** – review watering regime as your tree's uptake slows down, reduce watering as needed.
- **<u>Feeding</u>** - monitor feeding volume and frequency as trees begin to enter Autumn
- **<u>Pruning</u>** – continue pruning and trimming as necessary.
- **<u>Wiring</u>** –check for it biting in, reapply if necessary, and remove if no longer required
- **<u>Root Work</u>** – avoid unless emergency repotting.
- **<u>Pests & Diseases</u>** – periodically check your trees for any signs of ill health and pests.
- **<u>Shelter</u>** – be mindful of prolonged wet weather, ensure trees are not becoming waterlogged and cover as needed.
- **<u>Maintenance</u>** – a great time to prepare your display areas to take full advantage of your trees autumnal looks. If air layers have been applied later in the season, check for good root growth and cut them away from the parent tree and pot them up, otherwise, keep moist and leave until spring.

<u>**Northern Hemisphere**</u>

April

- <u>**Repotting**</u> – end of repotting season, monitor re-potted trees, aerate the soil of any non re-potted trees
- <u>**Watering**</u> – frequency increased with buds and leaves open, water in morning to avoid cold evening temperatures.
- <u>**Feeding**</u> - feed non re-potted trees that are in leaf, do not feed re-potted trees until the end of the month. Gently increase the feeding of your evergreens
- <u>**Pruning**</u> – light trimming can begin if the leaves have hardened off.
- <u>**Wiring**</u> –check for it biting in, reapply if necessary, and remove if no longer required
- <u>**Root Work**</u> – no root work required.
- <u>**Pests & Diseases**</u> – as temps increase, be extra vigilant to check for bugs and pests
- <u>**Shelter**</u> - cold frosty spells are still a danger, continue to protect your trees as necessary
- <u>**Maintenance**</u> – moss removal and general weeding needed as temps increase

Southern Hemisphere

April

- **Repotting** – emergency repotting only, begin planning for repotting season, stock up on soil and pots.
- **Watering** – monitor moisture levels carefully, trees can become waterlogged due to increased wet weather, less watering needed
- **Feeding** - cease feeding of deciduous trees as they enter dormancy, lightly feed evergreens and indoor tropical trees.
- **Pruning** – good time to review the image of your trees and make plans for future pruning. Trimming of tropical trees may continue as needed. Great time for structural pruning of evergreens.
- **Wiring** – good time to wire pines and set branches over winter, check existing wire, remove, or adjust if required.
- **Root Work** – no root work required unless there is a specific root related health concern
- **Pests & Diseases** – reduced threat as temperatures decrease, but remain vigilant and check regularly.
- **Shelter** – temperatures may start to begin to drop, take action to protect your trees from the cold and shelter from heavy rain if needed
- **Maintenance** –this is a good time to plant seeds. Also be extra mindful of waterlogged soil and root rot at this time of year if your trees aren't protected from the elements.

Northern Hemisphere

May

- **Repotting** – repotting season has passed, monitor re-potted trees and aerate the soil of non re-potted trees.
- **Watering** – with buds and leaves now open, water more frequently. Ideally in the morning at this stage to avoid cold evening temperatures.
- **Feeding** - feed non re-potted trees that are now in full leaf, you may now begin feeding last month's re-potted trees. Gently increase the feeding of your evergreens.
- **Pruning** – prune away any unwanted and dead branches on mature trees. Now is also a good time to prune younger, developing trees into your desired shape..
- **Wiring** –check for it biting in, reapply if necessary, and remove if no longer required
- **Root Work** – no root work required unless there is a specific root related health concern.
- **Pests & Diseases** – as temps increase, be extra vigilant to check for bugs and pests. Watch out for the formation of mildew and treat accordingly.
- **Shelter** – frosty spells are less of a danger but are still possible. Protect your trees accordingly.
- **Maintenance** – moss removal and general weeding needed as temps increase. Ensure any build up of green algae is cleaned from the pot or surface of the soil.

Southern Hemisphere

May

- **Repotting** – emergency repotting only, begin planning for repotting season, stock up on soil and pots.
- **Watering** – monitor moisture levels carefully, trees can become waterlogged due to increased wet weather, less watering needed
- **Feeding** - none required for deciduous and evergreens as trees have largely slowed down their growth or are now dormant, light feeding of indoor tropical trees may continue if needed
- **Pruning** – good time to review the image of your trees and make plans for future pruning. Trimming of tropical trees may continue as needed.
- **Wiring** – good time to wire pines and set branches over winter, also a good time to wire deciduous trees since they have shed their foliage. check existing wire, remove, and adjust if required.
- **Root Work** – no root work required unless there is a specific root related health concern.
- **Pests & Diseases** – reduced threat as temperatures have decreased but remain vigilant and check regularly.
- **Shelter** – with temperatures beginning to drop, take action to protect your trees from the colder weather and shelter from heavy rain if needed.
- **Maintenance** – sharpen tools, and stock up on supplies for the season ahead.

<u>**Northern Hemisphere**</u>

June

- <u>**Repotting**</u> – emergency repotting only
- <u>**Watering**</u> – monitor moisture levels carefully, increase watering to more than once per day if needed.
- <u>**Feeding**</u> - increase feeding volume and frequency on all trees now they are well into their growing season.
- <u>**Pruning**</u> – time to prune back any unwanted growth and maintain the shape with regular trimming.
- <u>**Wiring**</u> – New wiring not advised as foliage can be damaged. Check existing wire, adjust and remove if required.
- <u>**Root Work**</u> – no root work required unless there is a specific root related health concern.
- <u>**Pests & Diseases**</u> – as temperatures increase, be extra vigilant to check for bugs and pests, apply insecticide as needed. Remove any damaged or infected foliage or branches to avoid the risk of spreading.
- <u>**Shelter**</u> – heat and wind protection may now be a concern, ensure trees are shaded and secure as needed.
- <u>**Maintenance**</u> – great time to take cuttings for future propagation, ensure tools are sharp and clean, continue diligent moss removal and weeding.

Southern Hemisphere

June

- **Repotting** – emergency repotting only, begin planning for repotting season, stock up on soil and pots.
- **Watering** – monitor moisture levels carefully, trees can become waterlogged, due to increased wet weather less watering needed
- **Feeding** - none required as trees have largely slowed down their growth or are now dormant, light feeding of indoor tropical trees may continue if needed
- **Pruning** – good time to review the image of your trees and make plans for future pruning. Trimming of tropical trees may continue as needed.
- **Wiring** – no new wiring, check existing wiring, loosen or remove as required.
- **Root Work** – no root work required unless there is a specific root related health concern
- **Pests & Diseases** – reduced threat as temperatures decrease, but remain vigilant and check regularly
- **Shelter** – temperatures begin to drop, take action to protect your trees from the colder weather and shelter from heavy rain and freezing temperatures, ice and snow.
- **Maintenance** – sharpen tools, and stock up on supplies for the season ahead.

Northern Hemisphere

July

- **Repotting** – emergency repotting only
- **Watering** – monitor moisture levels carefully, increase watering to more than once per day if needed.
- **Feeding** - increase feeding volume and frequency on all trees now they are well into their growing season.
- **Pruning** – time to prune back any unwanted growth and maintain the shape with regular trimming.
- **Wiring** – Be careful when wiring as foliage can be damaged. Check existing wire, adjust and remove if required.
- **Root Work** – no root work required unless there is a specific root related health concern.
- **Pests & Diseases** – as temperatures increase, be extra vigilant to check for bugs and pests, apply insecticide as needed. Remove any damaged or infected foliage or branches to avoid the risk of spreading.
- **Shelter** – heat and wind protection may now be a concern, ensure trees are shaded and secure as needed.
- **Maintenance** – great time to take cuttings for future propagation, ensure tools are sharp and clean, continue diligent moss removal and weeding.

<u>**Southern Hemisphere**</u>

July

- <u>**Repotting**</u> – generally considered too early due to colder weather.
- <u>**Watering**</u> – due to the slow growth rate at this time of year watering will be required less frequently.
- <u>**Feeding**</u> - the vast majority of trees are still dormant, feeding is generally not required during the winter months.
- <u>**Pruning**</u> – ideal time to review your trees and plan for future pruning.
- <u>**Wiring**</u> –check for it biting in, reapply if necessary, and remove if no longer required
- <u>**Root Work**</u> – avoid unless emergency repotting.
- <u>**Pests & Diseases**</u> – periodically check your trees for any signs of ill health and pests.
- <u>**Shelter**</u> – continue to shelter your trees from potential freezing temperatures.
- <u>**Maintenance**</u> – sharpen tools, stock up on supplies for the season ahead.

<u>**Northern Hemisphere**</u>

August

- **<u>Repotting</u>** – emergency repotting only
- **<u>Watering</u>** – monitor moisture levels carefully, increase watering to more than once per day if needed.
- **<u>Feeding</u>** - maintain feeding volume and frequency as trees approach end of summer.
- **<u>Pruning</u>** – time to prune back any unwanted growth and maintain the shape with regular trimming.
- **<u>Wiring</u>** – Be careful when wiring as foliage can be damaged. Check existing wire, adjust and remove if required.
- **<u>Root Work</u>** – no root work required unless there is a specific root related health concern.
- **<u>Pests & Diseases</u>** – as temperatures increase, be extra vigilant to check for bugs and pests, apply insecticide as needed. Remove any damaged or infected foliage or branches to avoid the risk of spreading.
- **<u>Shelter</u>** – heat and wind protection may now be a concern, ensure trees are shaded and secure as needed.
- **<u>Maintenance</u>** – great time to take cuttings for future propagation, ensure tools are sharp and clean, continue diligent moss removal and weeding.

<u>**Southern Hemisphere**</u>

August

- <u>**Repotting**</u> – considered the best time to repot ahead of new buds forming in spring.
- <u>**Watering**</u> – continue to monitor and increase watering if required.
- <u>**Feeding**</u> – trees will soon start to awaken from dormancy, but it is considered too early to start a feeding regime at this early stage.
- <u>**Pruning**</u> – ideal time to review your trees and plan for future pruning.
- <u>**Wiring**</u> –check for it biting in, reapply if necessary, and remove if no longer required
- <u>**Root Work**</u> – root pruning will be required if considering repotting a specific tree this year. Please refer to the repotting chapter of this book
- <u>**Pests & Diseases**</u> – periodically check your trees for any new signs of ill health and pests.
- <u>**Shelter**</u> – continue to protect your tree from the elements and any cold snaps.
- <u>**Maintenance**</u> – prepare, clean and ready any pots to be used in advance.

Northern Hemisphere

September

- **Repotting** – emergency repotting only
- **Watering** – review watering regime as your tree's uptake slows down, reduce watering as needed.
- **Feeding** - monitor feeding volume and frequency as trees begin to enter Autumn
- **Pruning** – continue pruning and trimming as necessary.
- **Wiring** –check for it biting in, reapply if necessary, and remove if no longer required
- **Root Work** – avoid unless emergency repotting.
- **Pests & Diseases** – periodically check your trees for any signs of ill health and pests.
- **Shelter** – be mindful of prolonged wet weather, ensure trees are not becoming waterlogged and cover as needed.
- **Maintenance** – a great time to prepare your display areas to take full advantage of your trees autumnal looks. If air layers have been applied later in the season, check for good root growth and cut them away from the parent tree and pot them up, otherwise, keep moist and leave until spring.

<u>**Southern Hemisphere**</u>

September

- <u>**Repotting**</u> – now is the key time to repot if you haven't already started.
- <u>**Watering**</u> – frequency begins to increase due to the onset of the growing season.
- <u>**Feeding**</u> – small doses of fertilizer can be introduced to trees that have not been re-potted. Don't feed recently re-potted trees util they have had adequate time to recover. Approximately wait at least 3-4 weeks before applying any feed.
- <u>**Pruning**</u> – only carry out light pruning if necessary to avoid damaging new growth.
- <u>**Wiring**</u> –check for it biting in, reapply if necessary, and remove if no longer required
- <u>**Root Work**</u> – avoid removing large sections of root mass if structural pruning is required at this time..
- <u>**Pests & Diseases**</u> – periodically check your trees for any signs of ill health and pests.
- <u>**Shelter**</u> – continue to shelter your trees, beware of late frosts.
- <u>**Maintenance**</u> – check for and remove weeds and moss. Stock up on fertilizer.

Northern Hemisphere

October

- **Repotting** – emergency repotting only, begin planning for repotting season, stock up on soil and pots.
- **Watering** – monitor moisture levels carefully, trees can become waterlogged due to increased wet weather, less watering needed
- **Feeding** - cease feeding of deciduous trees as they enter dormancy, lightly feed evergreens and indoor tropical trees.
- **Pruning** – good time to review the image of your trees and make plans for future pruning. Trimming of tropical trees may continue as needed. Great time for structural pruning of evergreens.
- **Wiring** – good time to wire pines and set branches over winter, check existing wire, remove, or adjust if required.
- **Root Work** – no root work required unless there is a specific root related health concern
- **Pests & Diseases** – reduced threat as temperatures decrease, but remain vigilant and check regularly.
- **Shelter** – temperatures may start to begin to drop, take action to protect your trees from the cold and shelter from heavy rain if needed
- **Maintenance** –this is a good time to plant seeds. Also be extra mindful of waterlogged soil and root rot at this time of year if your trees aren't protected from the elements.

October

- **Repotting** – end of repotting season, monitor re-potted trees, aerate the soil of any non re-potted trees
- **Watering** – frequency increased with buds and leaves open, water in morning to avoid cold evening temperatures.
- **Feeding** - feed non re-potted trees that are in leaf, do not feed re-potted trees until the end of the month. Gently increase the feeding of your evergreens
- **Pruning** – light trimming can begin if the leaves have hardened off.
- **Wiring** –check for it biting in, reapply if necessary, and remove if no longer required
- **Root Work** – no root work required.
- **Pests & Diseases** – as temps increase, be extra vigilant to check for bugs and pests
- **Shelter** - cold frosty spells are still a danger, continue to protect your trees as necessary
- **Maintenance** – moss removal and general weeding needed as temps increase

Northern Hemisphere

November

- **Repotting** – emergency repotting only, begin planning for repotting season, stock up on soil and pots.
- **Watering** – monitor moisture levels carefully, trees can become waterlogged due to increased wet weather, less watering needed
- **Feeding** - none required for deciduous and evergreens as trees have largely slowed down their growth or are now dormant, light feeding of indoor tropical trees may continue if needed
- **Pruning** – good time to review the image of your trees and make plans for future pruning. Trimming of tropical trees may continue as needed.
- **Wiring** – good time to wire pines and set branches over winter, also a good time to wire deciduous trees since they have shed their foliage. check existing wire, remove, and adjust if required.
- **Root Work** – no root work required unless there is a specific root related health concern.
- **Pests & Diseases** – reduced threat as temperatures have decreased but remain vigilant and check regularly.
- **Shelter** – with temperatures beginning to drop, take action to protect your trees from the colder weather and shelter from heavy rain if needed.
- **Maintenance** – sharpen tools, and stock up on supplies for the season ahead.

November

- **Repotting** – repotting season has passed, monitor re-potted trees and aerate the soil of non re-potted trees.
- **Watering** – with buds and leaves now open, water more frequently. Ideally in the morning at this stage to avoid cold evening temperatures.
- **Feeding** - feed non re-potted trees that are now in full leaf, you may now begin feeding last month's re-potted trees. Gently increase the feeding of your evergreens.
- **Pruning** – prune away any unwanted and dead branches on mature trees. Now is also a good time to prune younger, developing trees into your desired shape..
- **Wiring** –check for it biting in, reapply if necessary, and remove if no longer required
- **Root Work** – no root work required unless there is a specific root related health concern.
- **Pests & Diseases** – as temps increase, be extra vigilant to check for bugs and pests. Watch out for the formation of mildew and treat accordingly.
- **Shelter** – frosty spells are less of a danger but are still possible. Protect your trees accordingly.
- **Maintenance** – moss removal and general weeding needed as temps increase. Ensure any build up of green algae is cleaned from the pot or surface of the soil.

December

- **Repotting** – emergency repotting only, begin planning for repotting season, stock up on soil and pots.
- **Watering** – monitor moisture levels carefully, trees can become waterlogged, due to increased wet weather less watering needed
- **Feeding** - none required as trees have largely slowed down their growth or are now dormant, light feeding of indoor tropical trees may continue if needed
- **Pruning** – good time to review the image of your trees and make plans for future pruning. Trimming of tropical trees may continue as needed.
- **Wiring** – no new wiring, check existing wiring, loosen or remove as required.
- **Root Work** – no root work required unless there is a specific root related health concern
- **Pests & Diseases** – reduced threat as temperatures decrease, but remain vigilant and check regularly
- **Shelter** – temperatures begin to drop, take action to protect your trees from the colder weather and shelter from heavy rain and freezing temperatures, ice and snow.
- **Maintenance** – sharpen tools, and stock up on supplies for the season ahead.

December

- **Repotting** – emergency repotting only
- **Watering** – monitor moisture levels carefully, increase watering to more than once per day if needed.
- **Feeding** - increase feeding volume and frequency on all trees now they are well into their growing season.
- **Pruning** – time to prune back any unwanted growth and maintain the shape with regular trimming.
- **Wiring** – New wiring not advised as foliage can be damaged. Check existing wire, adjust and remove if required.
- **Root Work** – no root work required unless there is a specific root related health concern.
- **Pests & Diseases** – as temperatures increase, be extra vigilant to check for bugs and pests, apply insecticide as needed. Remove any damaged or infected foliage or branches to avoid the risk of spreading.
- **Shelter** – heat and wind protection may now be a concern, ensure trees are shaded and secure as needed.
- **Maintenance** – great time to take cuttings for future propagation, ensure tools are sharp and clean, continue diligent moss removal and weeding.

GLOSSARY OF JAPANESE TERMS

- **Bonsai:** a miniature tree planted in a shallow pot.

- **Bunjingi:** the literati bonsai style where trees have slender trunks, contorted branches, and minimal foliage.

- **Chokkan:** the formal upright bonsai style where the tree trunk is upright and tapers.

- **Chu:** refers to its size, a bonsai tree that needs two hands to lift the pot.

- **Dai:** refers to its size, a bonsai tree that needs four hands, or two people, to lift the pot.

- **Fukinagashi:** the windswept bonsai style where it looks like the tree is exposed to wind from predominantly one direction, and branches and leaves only grow on one side of the trunk.

- **Han-kengai:** the semi-cascading bonsai style where the tree looks like it's growing on a cliff or riverbank.

- **Jin:** removal of the outer layer of bark to expose the smooth under-lying wood of a branch.

- **Kabudachi:** the multi-trunk bonsai style where three or more trunks grow from the same root system.

- **Keishi:** a thumb-sized bonsai tree, the smallest in tree size classification.

- **Kengai:** the cascading bonsai style where the tree is planted in a tall pot and the trunk is trained to grow downward.

- **Kifu Sho:** a bonsai tree up to 16 inches tall.

- **Mame:** a miniature bonsai tree up to 6 inches tall.

- **Misho:** growing a bonsai tree from seeds.

- **Moyogi:** the informal upright bonsai style where the trunk grows in a slight S-shape.

- **Seki-joju:** the on-a-rock bonsai style where the tree's roots seek out crevices in rock to find nutrients.

- **Shakan:** the slanting bonsai style where the trunk grows at a 60 to 80-degree angle to the ground.

- **Shari:** A technique used to remove large sections of the outer bark of the main trunk. Exposing the under-lying wood.

- **Shito:** a very small bonsai size reaching 3 inches tall.

- **Shohin:** a small bonsai size reaching up to 8 - 10 inches tall and the most popular bonsai size.

- **Sokan:** the double-trunk bonsai style where two trunks grow from one root system.

- **Yamadori:** small trees found in nature that are suitable for bonsai.

- **Yose-ue:** the forest bonsai style where multiple trees are grown in one pot.

REFERENCES

A beginner's guide to bonsai trees. (2018, August 24). Arborist Now. https://www.arboristnow.com/news/A-Beginner-s-Guide-to-Bonsai-Trees

A discussion on bonsai soil. (n.d.). All Things Bonsai. https://www.allthingsbonsai.co.uk/bonsai-tree-care/a-discussion-on-bonsai-soil/

A guide to watering bonsai. (n.d.). Bonsai 4 Me. http://bonsai4me.com/Basics/Basics_Watering.html

Akin, C. (2020a, May 17). *Your first bonsai tree: 4 things to know.* Bonsai Tree Resource Center. https://bonsairesourcecenter.com/4-things-you-need-to-know-before-buying-your-first-bonsai-tree/

Akin, C. (2020b, June 1). *The ultimate bonsai tree fertilizer beginner's guide.* Bonsai Tree Resource Center. https://bonsairesourcecenter.com/the-ultimate-bonsai-tree-fertilizer-beginners-guide/

Akin, C. (2020c, June 6). *How to identify 13 common bonsai pests & diseases.* Bonsai Tree Resource Center. https://bonsairesourcecenter.com/how-to-identify-13-common-bonsai-pests-diseases/

Akin, C. (2020d, June 6). *Know when to water your bonsai: 3 simple methods.* Bonsai Tree Resource Center. https://bonsairesourcecenter.com/know-when-to-water-your-bonsai-3-simple-methods/

Akin, C. (2020e, June 6). *The art of bonsai: 3 important lessons I learned from a bonsai tree.* Bonsai Tree Resource Center. https://bonsairesourcecenter.com/3-important-lessons-i-learned-from-a-bonsai-tree/

Akin, C. (2021, February 4). *6 easy steps to wire bonsai trees.* Bonsai Tree Resource Center. https://bonsairesource-center.com/6-easy-steps-to-wire-bonsai-tree/

Anushka. (2022, February 14). *Common Myths Related to Bonsai Plants.* Ferns N Petals. https://www.fnp.com/article/common-myths-related-to-bonsai-plants

Beginner bonsai: Two questions to ask yourself. (2020, November 16). Beechfield Bonsai. https://www.beechfieldbonsai.co.uk/beginner-bonsai-two-questions/

Bonsai: Caring & styling tips. (2018, May 28). MyBageecha. https://mybageecha.com/blogs/articles/bonsai-caring-styling-tips

Bonsai lifecycle. (n.d.). Kusamura Bonsai Club. https://www.kusamurabonsai.org/articles/bonsai-lifecycle/

Bonsai size classification chart and guide. (2019, September 12). Bonsai Sanctum. https://www.bonsaisanctum.com/bonsai-size-classification-chart-and-guide/

Bonsai soil, recommended substrate mixtures. (n.d.). Bonsai Empire. https://www.bonsaiempire.com/basics/bonsai-care/bonsai-soil

Bonsai styles, shapes and forms. (n.d.). Bonsai Empire. https://www.bonsaiempire.com/origin/bonsai-styles

Bonsai styling. (n.d.). Bonsai Shop. https://www.bonsai-shop.com/en/styling

Bonsai tools and supplies explained! Beginner & advanced tools. (2021, April 4). Terrarium Planting Guide. https://plantinterrarium.com/bonsai-tools-and-supplies-explained-beginner-advanced-tools/

Bonsai tree diseases - how to treat bonsai health issues. (n.d.). Bonsai and Blooms. https://www.bonsai-and-blooms.com/bonsai-tree-diseases.html

Bonsai tree pests - how to protect your trees. (n.d.). Bonsai and Blooms. https://www.bonsai-and-blooms.com/bonsai-tree-pests.html

Buying bonsai trees in a store or online shop. (n.d.). Bonsai Empire. https://www.bonsaiempire.com/basics/cultivation/buying-bonsai

Buying nursery stock (prebonsai). (n.d.). Bonsai Empire. https://www.bonsaiempire.com/basics/cultivation/nursery-stock

Collecting trees from the forest (yamadori). (n.d.). Bonsai Empire. https://www.bonsaiempire.com/basics/cultivation/collecting-trees

Deciduous conifers. (2016). Lake Wilderness Arboretum. https://www.lakewildernessarboretum.org/gardens/legacy-garden/deciduous-conifers/

Definition and meaning of bonsai. (2019). Bonsai Empire. https://www.bonsaiempire.com/origin/what-is-bonsai

Del Castillo, R. (2018, September 22). *How to use fertilizer to grow your bonsai tree*. Bonsai Tree Gardener. https://www.bonsaitreegardener.net/care/feeding-fertilizer

Detailed history of bonsai. (2019). Bonsai Boy Catalog. https://www.bonsaiboy.com/catalog/historyofbonsai.html

Dupuich, J. (2017, September 5). *How to care for bonsai during heat waves*. Bonsai Tonight. https://bonsaitonight.com/2017/09/05/how-to-care-for-bonsai-during-heat-waves/

Exploding 5 myths around bonsai trees. (2021, July 31). Yorkshire Bonsai. https://www.yorkshirebonsai.co.uk/blogs/advice-guides/exploding-5-myths-around-bonsai-trees

Fall and winter bonsai tree care. (2023, January 2). My Garden Life. https://mygardenlife.com/garden-tips/fall-and-winter-bonsai-tree-care

Fathame, R. (2022, August 31). *Carbon steel vs stainless steel bonsai tools.* Live with Bonsai. https://bonsaitricks.com/carbon-steel-vs-stainless-steel-bonsai-tools/

Fertilizing 101: How to fertilize your bonsai. (2019, February 13). Bonsai Sanctum. https://www.bonsaisanctum.com/fertilize-bonsai/

Fertilizing bonsai, feeding is crucial for trees. (n.d.). Bonsai Empire. https://www.bonsaiempire.com/basics/bonsai-care/fertilizing

5 wiring tips for your bonsai trees. (2017, March 29). Bonsai Tree (Pty) Ltd. https://www.bonsaitree.co.za/blogs/tree-talk/5-top-wiring-tips-for-your-bonsai-trees

Grow trees from seed as bonsai cultivation technique. (2019). Bonsai Empire. https://www.bonsaiempire.com/basics/cultivation/from-seeds

Growing bonsai from seed - the pros and cons. (n.d.). Bonsai and Blooms. https://www.bonsai-and-blooms.com/growing-bonsai-from-seed.html

Harrington, H. (2021). *BONSAI: Collecting trees from the wild part one.* Bonsai 4 Me. http://bonsai4me.com/AdvTech/ATcollec-tring%20trees%20from%20the%20wild%20W%20Pall.htm

Healing wounds on bonsai trees. (n.d.). Back Garden Bonsai. https://www.backgardenbonsai.com/healing-wounds-on-bonsai-trees/

History of bonsai. (2019). Bonsai Empire. https://www.bonsaiempire.com/origin/bonsai-history

How to keep your bonsai safe in summer. (2022, July 19). Bonsai 2 U. https://bonsai2u.co.uk/how-to-keep-your-bonsai-safe-in-summer/

How to water bonsai when on vacation? (2022, August 27). Bonsai Express. https://www.bonsai-express.com/bonsai-care/how-to-water-bonsai-when-on-vacation

Javier, S. (2022, February 14). *4 plant watering methods: Which is best for my plants?* Unbeleafable. https://unbeleafable.ph/plant-watering-methods

Meservy, M. (2021, September 23). *Simple ways to revive a bonsai tree: 13 steps (with pictures).* WikiHow. https://www.wikihow.com/Revive-a-Bonsai-Tree

Nakamura, A. (2018a, September 22). *Bonsai tree size classifi-cations*. Bonsai Tree Gardener. https://www.bonsaitree-gardener.net/general/size-classification

Nakamura, A. (2018b, September 22). *How to position your bonsai tree*. Bonsai Tree Gardener. https://www.bon-saitreegardener.net/care/how-to/position

Nakamura, A. (2018c, October 2). *How to cultivate the roots of a bonsai tree*. Bonsai Tree Gardener. https://www.bon-saitreegardener.net/care/how-to/roots

Nakamura, A. (2022, December 25). *Busting 10 common myths about bonsai*. Bonsai Tree Gardener. https://www.bon-saitreegardener.net/bonsai-trees/busting-10-common-myths-about-bonsai

Nathan Andersen. (n.d.). *Fundamentals of bonsai - stages of bonsai*. Nate's Nursery. https://www.natesnursery.com/fundamentals-of-bonsai-stages-of-bonsai/

Nicass, F. (2021, June 24). *What is bonsai ramification? Bonsai ramification explained*. Plant Paladin. https://plantpala-din.com/bonsai-ramification/

Nicass, F. (2022, November 14). *Bonsai pot vs ground - an in-depth guide*. Plant Paladin. https://plantpaladin.com/bon-sai-pot-vs-ground/

Nickson, J. (2019, October 8). *The ultimate bonsai style chart.* Grow Your Bonsai. https://growyourbonsai.com/the-ulti-mate-bonsai-style-chart-with-pictures-details/

Nickson, J. (2020, April 6). *The ultimate guide to watering your bonsai tree.* Grow Your Bonsai. https://growyourbon-sai.com/the-ultimate-guide-to-watering-your-bonsai-tree/

O'Neill, T. (2022, July 21). *The ultimate guide to bonsai repot-ting.* Simplify Gardening. https://simplifygarden-ing.com/guide-to-bonsai-repotting/

Paula. (2021, December 24). *Creating your bonsai soil at home | helpful tips & insight.* Bonsai Gardener. https://www.bonsaigardener.org/creating-your-bonsai-soil-at-home

Poem: Tall oaks from little acorns grow by David Everett. (n.d.). Poetry Nook. https://www.poetrynook.com/poem/tall-oaks-little-acorns-grow

Potter, G. (2005). *Using seaweed products in bonsai cultiva-tion.* Kaizen Bonsai. https://www.kaizenbonsai.com/bon-sai-tree-care-information/using-seaweed-products-in-bon-sai-cultivation

Prachi, P. (2022, July 17). *Bonsai pots: The ultimate guide for beginners.* Abana Homes. https://abanahomes.com/bon-sai-pot-guide

Preparing your bonsai trees for winter. (n.d.). All Things Bonsai. https://www.allthingsbonsai.co.uk/bonsai-tree-care/preparing-your-bonsai-trees-for-winter/

Pruning bonsai, cutting branches to shape the tree. (2019). Bonsai Empire. https://www.bonsaiempire.com/basics/styling/pruning

Requirements of bonsai soils. (n.d.). Bonsai Empire. https://www.bonsaiempire.com/blog/bonsai-soil-requirements

Sakurako. (2022, November 26). *Should you protect bonsai from rain?* Bonsai Station. https://bonsaistation.com/protect-bonsai-from-rain/

Sears, C. (2022, August 23). *9 popular types of bonsai trees.* The Spruce. https://www.thespruce.com/popular-types-of-bonsai-trees-5025687

7 signs for a healthy tree. (2018, April 12). Longacre Tree Surgery. https://longacretreesurgery.co.uk/7-signs-for-a-healthy-tree/

Stockton, J. (2014, March 20). *How to pick a pre-bonsai or nursery plant: Step by step guide.* Grow a Bonsai Tree. https://www.growabonsaitree.com/propagation/pre-bonsai

Taggart, E. (2021, March 6). *Behold the bonsai: Learn the ancient history and meaning of this miniature tree.* My Modern Met. https://mymodernmet.com/bonsai-tree-history/

The 2 stages of bonsai. (2021, March 22). Bonsai EN. https://www.bonsai-en.com.au/post/the-2-stages-of-bonsai

The tree guide at arborday.org. (2019). Arbor Day Foundation. https://www.arborday.org/trees/treeGuide/anatomy.cfm

The why and when of repotting your bonsai trees. (n.d.-a). Bonsai Tree (Pty) Ltd. https://www.bonsaitree.co.za/blogs/tree-talk/55461187-the-why-and-when-of-repotting-your-bonsai-trees

The why and when of repotting your bonsai trees. (n.d.-b). Bonsai Tree (Pty) Ltd. https://www.bonsaitree.co.za/blogs/tree-talk/55461187-the-why-and-when-of-repotting-your-bonsai-trees

Watering bonsai while away or on holiday - guide. (2020, March 29). Gardener's Yards. https://gardenersyards.com/watering-bonsai-while-away-or-on-holiday/

What is anodizing? The finish of choice. (2018). Anodizing.org. https://www.anodizing.org/page/what-is-anodizing

What is the best bonsai tree for beginners? (n.d.). All Things Bonsai. https://www.allthingsbonsai.co.uk/bonsai-tree-care/what-is-the-best-bonsai-tree-for-beginners/

When do you remove the wire from your bonsai? (n.d.). Back Garden Bonsai. https://www.backgardenbonsai.com/when-do-you-remove-the-wire-from-your-bonsai/

Where to place your bonsai tree. (n.d.). Bonsai Empire. https://www.bonsaiempire.com/basics/bonsai-care/position

Wiring bonsai. (n.d.). Bonsai Shop. https://www.bonsai-shop.com/en/styling/wiring

Yui, T. (2020, October 27). *Bonsai wind protection.* Wazakura Japan. https://wazakurajapan.com/blogs/news/wind-protection

Image References

Adobe Stock Illustrations and Vector Assets– Fully Licensed by RJ Publishings Ltd – RS & JN

All other Illustrations created and owned by RJ Publishings Ltd

Arāja, E. (2020). Bonsai on White Background [Online Image]. In *Pexels.* https://www.pexels.com/photo/bonsai-on-white-background-4050790/

Bishop, J. (2019). Green-leafed Tree [Online Image]. In *Pexels.* https://www.pexels.com/photo/green-leafed-tree-2422916/

csk. (2022). bonsai pine tree pine bonsai nature [Online Image]. In *Pixabay*. https://pixabay.com/photos/bonsai-pine-tree-pine-bonsai-nature-7271257/

Finardi, L. (2021). Bonsai plant pot tree leaves [Online Image]. In *Pixabay*. https://pixabay.com/photos/bonsai-plant-pot-tree-leaves-6114252/

Fox, K. (2018). Selective focus photography of bonsai plant photo [Online Image]. In *Unsplash*. https://unsplash.com/photos/gsU5hLEg1vA?utm_source=unsplash&utm_medium=referral&utm_content=creditShareLink

Goellner, A. (2020). Gardening Work Table Tool [Online Image]. In *Pixabay*. https://pixabay.com/photos/gardening-work-table-tool-4892083/

Heftiba, T. (2017). Green leafed plant photography photo [Online Image]. In *Unsplash*. https://unsplash.com/photos/W1yjvf5idqA

Hempel, P. (2016). Bonsai juniper [Online Image]. In *Pixabay*. https://pixabay.com/photos/bonsai-juniper-moon-shell-nature-1183558/

Ilyés, I. (2016). Bonsai pine plant culture artistic [Online Image]. In *Pixabay*. https://pixabay.com/photos/bonsai-pine-plant-culture-artistic-1805501/

Ilyés, I. (2019). Bonsai trees plants [Online Image]. In *Pixabay*. https://pixabay.com/photos/bonsai-trees-plants-4634225/

Ilyés, I. (2021). Bonsai snow snowfall winter plant [Online Image]. In *Pixabay*. https://pixabay.com/photos/bonsai-snow-snowfall-winter-plant-6117619/

Ilyés, I. (2022). Azalea bonsai wood flowers [Online Image]. In *Pixabay*. https://pixabay.com/photos/azalea-bonsai-wood-flowers-7101128/

Kang, S. (2020). Potted green bonsai plant on table [Online Image]. In *Pexels*. https://www.pexels.com/photo/potted-green-bonsai-plant-on-table-6045734/

Nekrashevich, A. (2021). A metal watering can on a countertop [Online Image]. In *Pexels*. https://www.pexels.com/photo/a-metal-watering-can-on-a-countertop-8989429/

Nguyen Vinh, Q. (2022a). Bonsai tree with flowers [Online Image]. In *Pexels*. https://www.pexels.com/photo/bonsai-tree-with-flowers-12739173/

Nguyen Vinh, Q. (2022b). Wood bench landscape summer [Online Image]. In *Pexels*. https://www.pexels.com/photo/wood-bench-landscape-summer-14771841/

scartmyart. (2018). Wood tree plant [Online Image]. In *Pixabay*. https://pixabay.com/photos/wood-tree-plant-ceramics-bonsai-3441147/

Shaheer, M. (2021, February 12). *Red and green plant on blue ceramic pot photo*. Unsplash. https://unsplash.com/photos/2Bk_gsQGLGg?utm_source=unsplash&utm_medium=referral&utm_content=creditShareLink

Srithakae, P. (2022). Green plant in white ceramic pot [Online Image]. In *Pexels*. https://www.pexels.com/photo/green-plant-in-white-ceramic-pot-11007019/

Waldl, A. (2019). Potted plant sapling green [Online Image]. In *Pixabay*. https://pixabay.com/photos/potted-plant-sapling-green-4110329/

Made in the USA
Monee, IL
14 July 2024